HISTORIC
BADDECK

JOCELYN BETHUNE

NIMBUS
PUBLISHING

For Robin, Marc, and Jonathan

Nimbus Publishing Limited
PO Box 9166, Halifax, NS B3K 5M8
(902) 455-4286 www.nimbus.ca

Printed and bound in Canada

Typesetting: Jesse Marchand
Cover design: Heather Bryan

Library and Archives Canada Cataloguing in Publication

Bethune, Jocelyn
Historic Baddeck / Jocelyn Bethune.

ISBN 978-1-55109-706-0

1. Baddeck (N.S.)—History. 2. Baddeck (N.S.)—Biography. I. Title.

FC2349.B34B47 2009   971.6'93   C2008-907173-5

We acknowledge the financial support of the Government of Canada through the Book Publishing Industry Development Program (BPIDP) and the Canada Council, and of the Province of Nova Scotia through the Department of Tourism, Culture and Heritage for our publishing activities.

Contents

Acknowledgements

The first time I walked down the main street of Baddeck in April 1987, I knew I had come home. I felt as though my soul had always resided here. I wanted to know more about the people that settled here, the businesses they built, how they lived their lives. Soon afterward, I met my husband, Norman, and he introduced me to his late grandfather's photo collection. We often pored over the photos, discovering details about life in Baddeck within the sepia photographs. Since then, Norman has encouraged my desire to publish a Baddeck history. He has always been beside me—conducting research, gathering photos, offering sound judgment and advice, and editing each draft. My heartfelt gratitude to him for his enduring encouragement and support.

I am thankful for the many days spent at the home of my in-laws, Normie and Muriel Bethune, drinking tea in their sunroom, looking through old photos and newspaper clippings. Over two decades, those visits introduced me to the colourful people and the long gone (but not forgotten) businesses that have made this history-filled village special. Many of the photos and research materials are courtesy of my father-in-law.

Joan MacInnes proves everyday that having an archivist on staff is a vital part of the workings of Victoria County. She is a fount of information, with knowledge about the buildings of the county and the people who inhabited them. I thank her for reviewing the manuscript and for her quick responses to my many questions.

Thanks to doctors Drew and Graeme Bethune for generously sharing their collection of papers, photos, and books gathered over the years by their great-uncle, Dr. Clarence Bethune, and his mother, Mary Jones Bethune.

In true Cape Breton form, there are two James MacDonalds to thank—"Carpenter" Jim (who is also an author and historian) for reviewing the manuscript, for his encouragement, and for sharing research gems and photos; and "Building Supplies" James (also a carpenter) for sharing his in-depth knowledge of Sam Cunard Campbell and Baddeck people and their boats.

I am grateful to Donnell and Betty Beaton for the delightful chats at their kitchen table and for sharing their photo collection and research materials; to Nancy Langley for a tea party at Wong's (the

New Bras d'Or House) and for details about the White Store; and to Lloyd Stone, for his conversations about Baddeck history and for taking care of Knox Cemetery.

At the Alexander Graham Bell National Historic Site of Canada, my thanks to Aynsley MacFarlane for reading the Bell chapter, Sharon Morrow for help finding photos, and my co-worker Donna Johnson for reading the Bell chapter (and for all the laughs); Anne MacNeil, Anne Connell, and Jane Arnold at the Beaton Institute at Cape Breton University; the helpful staff at the Public Archives of Nova Scotia; Laverne McRae and Kate Oland at the Baddeck Public Library; Robert Morgan, Bonnie Thornhill, Fraser MacLeod, Carole MacDonald, Peggy Morrison, Linda Murphy, Shirley Kerr, Juanita MacAulay, Charles and Rannie Blanchard, Margie Crowdis, Bev Dunlop, Sean Dunlop, Muriel Carmichael, Linda MacIvor, Gordon MacAulay Sr., Liz MacNeil, Penny Chapman, Jonena MacLeod, Wilf Tremaine, James Fraser, Wayne and Anne Kerr, Lyn and Gerald Dunlop, and Judi and Bernie MacDonald for generously sharing research materials, information, and photographs. Thanks to my parents, Lexie and Gordon Reid and to Simone Carmichael, Pam Ellsworth, and Stacey Pineau for providing morale boosts always at the right time; to Patrick Murphy and Jesse Marchand at Nimbus, patient and helpful editors; and to Jane Buss, director of the Writers' Federation of Nova Scotia, for her helpful suggestions, timely advice, and frequent encouragements.

Should any errors or omissions be noted, please contact the author at jbethune@ns.sympatico.ca.

Introduction

It is July 4, 2008, and the sky over Kidston Island is alight with red, white, and blue. The pyrotechnic display of pinwheel spirals and rocket splays is part of a special celebration to mark one hundred years since the lakeside village was incorporated, and is a tribute to the American friends who have called Baddeck home.

Although Alexander Graham Bell is often the first name that comes to mind, a century before the telephone inventor stepped onto the Baddeck shore, another man from south of the border found his way here.

The beginnings of a permanent settlement near Baddeck, Nova Scotia, can be traced back to 1777, to the ruins of a burned-out home during the American War of Independence. There, on the banks of the Hudson River in Upstate New York, in that smouldering wreckage of a fire deliberately set, Jonathan Jones lost his home, his business, his most treasured possessions, and his sense of belonging.

In the days before the outbreak of hostilities in 1775, Jones, a married father of four children, enjoyed a quiet life near Glens Falls, sixty-five kilometres north of Albany. His widowed mother, six brothers, and sister, who lived nearby, were described as upstanding and pioneering citizens. Jones was an entrepreneur who grew crops for sale and owned a water-powered gristmill and sawmill. As a justice of the peace, he upheld and administered the laws of the colony.

But the war turned that world upside down. It pitted neighbour against neighbour and divided families. The Jones brothers were among many branded "obnoxious Tories." They refused to take an oath of allegiance to the rebel Patriots, and their scorched lands were confiscated and sold. Jonathan's brothers, Dunham and Thomas, died during the bloody battles that followed. Another brother, David, a lieutenant in the British Army, was engaged to Jane McCrae, a pretty twenty-year-old neighbour of the Jones family. She was brutally murdered on their wedding day. In a tragic and ironic twist, her death rallied the Patriot cause. Her story became the stuff of American folklore, and she was hailed as a Revolutionary War heroine. Jonathan, a captain in the King's Loyal American Rangers, was wounded at Saratoga, a pivotal battle that brought the French into the hostilities, bolstering the American side with food, funds, ships, and troops.

Soon after, Jonathan Jones and his family left America forever. His wife, Sarah (Samson) Jones, gave birth to their fifth child while the family was encamped at Sorel, Quebec. His elderly mother and four of his brothers were among the first settlers in Maitland, near Brockville, Ontario. But Jonathan took his family east, to the wild, mostly unpopulated island of Cape Breton. By 1785, he was living in the ruins at Louisbourg with a handful of other Loyalist refugees.

MOUTH OF THE BADDECK RIVER, C.1930. IN THE 1780S, JONATHAN JONES SETTLED ON THE BANKS OF THE BADDECK RIVER, A LOCATION ABOUT EIGHT KILOMETRES WEST OF THE PRESENT-DAY VILLAGE, MARKING THE FIRST PERMANENT SETTLEMENT IN THE BADDECK AREA.

As a reward for his loyalty, the British granted him one thousand acres on the Bras d'Or Lake, with additional acreage in Sydney. He began to clear a spot on the banks of the Baddeck River, where he built a home for his waiting family. Within a decade, he had a thriving farm with almost one hundred cattle, sheep, a small gristmill, and a sawmill.

"You see how we live here," he wrote in a letter to his brother Solomon in March 1797, "separated from all the world, a little republic of our own. I sometimes think we are as happy as though we were in the hurry and bustle of company. The children are all well. I am happy to have it in my power to tell you that they constitute the principal part of the pleasure that I enjoy or ever expect to enjoy in this life."

Not far away, at the mouth of the *Ebadek* river, the Mi'kmaq fished for trout and salmon. While *Ebadek* has been defined as the "place with island nearby" and the "place where river runs parallel to the lake," an 1875 Mi'kmaq language handbook defines it simply as "a sultry place." Soon *Ebadek* became Baddeck with the name describing the developing settlement on the river.

The Mi'kmaq people, hunters and gatherers, had lived along the shores of the Bras d'Or for thousands of years. Beneath the waters of the lake there is evidence of early native settlements, where these peoples lived in abundant river valleys before a sudden catastrophic event some six thousand years ago caused the Atlantic Ocean to rush in, turning the valley into the floor of an inland sea.

A MI'KMAQ ENCAMPMENT NEAR ENGLISHTOWN, C.1880

The Mi'kmaq navigated the vast inland waterway by canoe, camping near estuaries that fed the lake, which they called *Petoo'bok* ("a long dish of salt water"). The women of the nomadic tribe disassembled their wigwams in the fall for the annual trek to St. Peters, on the southwestern shore of the lake.

When Samuel Holland conducted a survey of the lake in 1765 he noted that the Mi'kmaq "behaved very peaceably. But seemed dissatisfied at the Lake being surveyed—saying we had discovered now all their private haunts."

By the time Jonathan Jones penned his last will and testament in 1808, boatloads of Scottish highlanders were en route to settle in the nearby hills and vales. Within a decade, they increased the population of Cape Breton from two thousand to almost ten thousand people.

With an eye for opportunity, James Duffus, brother-in-law of shipping magnate Samuel Cunard, arrived in 1819. Cunard knew of the influx of Scottish Highlanders to Cape Breton, and encouraged Duffus to build a business there. Duffus and his wife, Margaret, settled on a little island in the Bras d'Or. He named it Duke of Kent Island and established a successful trade with the nearby communities of Middle River, Big Bras d'Or, and Boularderie. An eight-kilometre footpath through the woods linked the community at the Baddeck River to the mainland shore near Duffus's store, and a canoe was used to ferry customers across the narrow channel to the store.

When Duffus died suddenly at age forty, William Kidston arrived to clear the estate. His widow Margaret Duffus married Kidston two years later and he assumed title to the Duffus land grant, which included the island and four hundred acres opposite it. The slice of land first settled by Duffus then became known as Kidston Island.

Soon, Joseph Campbell settled on the mainland shore, and was the first to settle in the present day location of the village of Baddeck. He established a way house where weary travellers from Middle River and the Margarees could rest overnight before continuing on their journeys to Big Bras d'Or and the Sydneys. Campbell sold his valuable waterfront property on a cove at the western end of the village to James Anderson for a barrel of oatmeal. This burgeoning community was called Little Baddeck to distinguish it from its older, more populated riverside neighbour to the west.

Lawyer Alfred Haliburton lobbied to see that Baddeck, population forty-five, was selected as the seat for the newly formed Victoria County in 1851. (Until 1851, "Baddeck" referred to the community that is now known as Big Baddeck, and the present-day village was called Little Baddeck. In this book, "Baddeck" is used in the contemporary sense.) As a result, a courthouse was built on the newly surveyed main street. David and Catherine Dunlop arrived from Newfoundland in the late 1850s. David was the superintendent of the overland telegraph cable project that would link Newfoundland with Cape Breton. Catherine saw potential in the developing town for a boarding house with a telegraph office. By the 1860s the Dunlops had constructed the Telegraph House, one of the first businesses built on Chebucto Street, steps away from the courthouse. When American writer Charles Dudley Warner stumbled into the hotel after a long wagon ride in the early 1870s, the Dunlop family's legendary hospitality greeted him. His travelogue, *Baddeck and That Sort of Thing*, extolled the virtues of this blissfully quiet town, securing the picturesque village's reputation as a tourist destination.

TELEGRAPH HOUSE, 1958

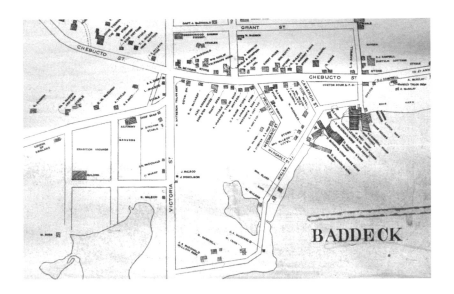

MAP OF BADDECK,
c.1885

Future entrepreneur and politician Charles J. Campbell began his career working at Kidston's Island Store. He created a successful ship-building industry on Baddeck's waterfront. His political ties in Ottawa secured the construction of a post office and customs house on the village's main street in 1885. A stone carving of his face, placed at the all-important keystone above the entrance, ensured that his success was remembered.

Robert Elmsley was a teenager when he arrived in Baddeck in 1840 from Scotland. He worked side by side with Charles Campbell at Kidston's store. His diary of everyday jottings from 1855 to 1889 provides a rare glimpse into the daily comings and goings in the lakeside village. His concise entries note when the stoves are first fired up in the church, when the ice is passable, marriages, births, and deaths.

In September of 1885, as a produce-filled cart rolls along the dusty main street, a farmer with a Scottish lilt calls out a Gaelic greeting. Doors are propped open at the mercantile shops that line Chebucto Street, while busy women bustle in and out. In the distance, the sound of carpenters hammering pegs into the frame of the new Greenwood church can be heard. The little village is thriving when Alexander Graham Bell steps off the steamer *Marion* at the busy waterfront wharf on that late summer day, marking a new era in the village's history. While other events helped shape the course of the village, none were as influential as the arrival of the Bell family that September.

Simply having a world-famous inventor living in the community would have been enough to bring attention to Baddeck. But Bell continued to invent after moving to Baddeck, so new groundbreaking technologies were introduced to the world from the tiny village on the edge of the continent. Huge kites, a twenty-one-metre- (seventy-foot-)

ALEXANDER GRAHAM
BELL ADDRESSES THE
CROWD AT THE GRAND
OPENING OF THE
TETRAHEDRAL TOWER
ATOP BEINN BHREAGH
MOUNTAIN ON AUGUST
31, 1907. MABEL
BELL STANDS AT THE
FOOT OF THE STAIRS;
BEHIND HER ARE THE
BELLS' GRANDSON
MELVILLE GROSVENOR
AND CASEY BALDWIN.

BELOW

HOMES ON WATER
STREET, BACK VIEW,
C.1920

high tripod lookout tower, the first powered flight in Canada, and the fastest boat in the world were among the many innovations born in Baddeck through Alexander Graham Bell's presence.

But Alexander Graham and Mabel Bell brought more than scientific firsts to the village—they also brought progressive ideas that changed the way people thought. Mabel Bell rallied parents to become involved in their children's education and helped residents create the first home and school association in Canada. She assisted in the development of a public library, the first on Cape Breton Island and only the second in the province in 1891. She and her husband frequently donated encyclopedias, annals, and novels to the library, a building she owned and allowed the community to use free of charge.

In the 1930s Casey Baldwin touted the benefits of a looping highway around northern Cape Breton with its start and finish in Baddeck. Baldwin, a Toronto-born mechanical engineer, came to Baddeck to work with Bell in 1907. As a Member of Parliament for Victoria County, Baldwin campaigned for the formation of Cape Breton Highlands National Park and the development of the Cabot Trail. His efforts sprouted other attractions, including the Gaelic College of Celtic Arts at St. Ann's, and in 1956, the Alexander Graham Bell National Historic Site, a museum dedicated to the inventor, at Baddeck. Near the end of the twentieth century Bell Bay Golf Club, a world-class eighteen-hole course, was carved from the sloping hill overlooking the Bras d'Or.

In 2008, as the village celebrated its centennial, a new development was on the way—a modern seniors' home on Shore Road.

Today, Baddeck retains many of the buildings and homes that graced the community one hundred years ago. Modern-day phone books include both the family names of the town's pioneering peoples as well as newer arrivals. Each person that lives here leaves his or her imprint. As William Shakespeare wrote, "There is history in all men's lives."

Chapter 1

Business and Industry

TELEGRAPH HOUSE, c.1900

F rom its perch on the upper side of Chebucto Street, this stately
federal-style hotel, built around 1860, has been a beacon for visitors and a cornerstone of Cape Breton's tourism industry.

Built when Baddeck's main industry was shipbuilding and the
telegraph was the fastest means of long-distance communication, the
Telegraph House has stood witness to the ebb and flow of life on the
main street of Baddeck.

The inn was the vision of Catherine (McGrath) Dunlop, a feisty Newfoundlander who immediately recognized the potential of the small but growing town when she arrived in the late 1850s. Her Scottish-born husband, David, was superintendent of the company laying telegraph cables across Newfoundland and Nova Scotia. The Dunlop family followed the cable to Cape Breton, where it was winding its way from Cape North to Port Hastings, bringing with it "instantaneous" communication. Because of its central location, Baddeck was an ideal spot for the Dunlops to build a boarding house—complete, of course, with a telegraph office.

When New England writer Charles Dudley Warner arrived, straggling into the village under a starlit sky, fifteen years later, he wrote of being received by a family "at the door of a very unhotel-like appearing hotel. It had a front flower garden; it was blazing with welcome lights; it opened hospitable doors."

During his stay, Warner luxuriated in undisturbed sleep, ate a delicious home-cooked meal on the balcony, and watched as the full moon rose over the point of Red Head to glisten on the waters of the Bras d'Or. The 1874 publication of Warner's travelogue, *Baddeck and that Sort of Thing*, cemented the village's reputation as a tourist destination.

A decade later, when telephone inventor Alexander Graham Bell and his family were making plans to travel to Cape Breton and Newfoundland, Bell read Warner's book and decided to make a brief stopover in Baddeck. Mabel Bell recalled in 1918 that it was the welcome shown to her family by Catherine Dunlop so many years before that "induced us to make Baddeck our summer home."

Bradalbane, a 224-ton barque, was the largest vessel built in Baddeck. Built by politician and entrepreneur Charles J. Campbell, it was launched from the Baddeck waterfront in 1854 with a flourish when Campbell's wife Eliza christened the ship, breaking a bottle of wine on the boat's bow. It was an elaborate ship with fittings imported from Scotland. Named for its owner's Scottish clan, the Campbells of Bradalbane, its maiden voyage took Charles back to his homeland on a business trip. In 1857, the vessel was one of six to take eight hundred followers of Reverend Norman McLeod from St. Ann's and Baddeck to New Zealand.

Over the next thirty years, the Baddeck waterfront saw the building and launching of more than thirty vessels, many of them by Charles Campbell. Robert Elmsley notes in his diary that after Campbell built a small log house and a store on the mainland, he supervised the crafting of *The Highlander*, a trade vessel built to carry livestock, foodstuffs, and lumber from Big Baddeck, Middle River, and the Margarees to ports beyond. While there had previously been other boats built in Baddeck, this fifty-five-ton schooner marked the beginning of a sustainable industry.

Baddeck prospered with each ship that was built and launched. Businesses soon established themselves on the newly created main street. What had started as a settlement with a handful of families in a few scattered homes in 1851 had blossomed into a village of almost

1,800 people just twenty years later. By 1875, a lighthouse was built at the eastern end of Kidston's Island, providing a beacon to welcome ships into the harbour.

The shipbuilding era ended in 1883 when the *Glenarchy*, the last ship built for trade, glided into the Bras d'Or. Other boats were built here, however. Master craftsman Walter Pinaud built boats for Alexander Graham Bell, including the sleek yawl *Elsie,* and Casey Baldwin's record-holding yacht, *Typhoon*. Pinaud opened his own boatyard in Baddeck in 1926.

The Pinaud-designed *Elsie* (1917) would for generations come to symbolize the pure joy of sailing on the Bras d'Or. Within a few years of the yacht's construction, William Nutting, Casey Baldwin, and Gilbert Grosvenor would create the Cruising Club of America on *Elsie's* decks as the boat sailed near Baddeck in the summer of 1922.

THE FIRST BRAS D'OR HOUSE, C.1890

The first Bras d'Or House hotel was built in the 1860s. The two-and-a-half-storey colonial-style building was destroyed by fire in October 1894.

The fire struck just as the Young Ladies Club of Baddeck was about to host an antique expo at the Masonic Hall. A number of the antiques were stored at the hotel. In a letter to her mother, Mabel Bell described how the fire affected one woman who had brought antiques to be displayed:

> I think we shall have a lot of things [at the expo] if people aren't scared by the fire, which burned up some [antiques that]…Miss Cain got for us in Middle River. They were all in her room at the Bras d'Or House and it burnt to the ground in less than no time. She only came back that day and carefully carried the things up to her room for safekeeping, but a half an hour before. If she had left them downstairs they would have escaped [as] all the downstairs furniture was saved, everything almost but Miss Cain's things. The fire made a clean sweep of those things including every penny she had in the world.

Alex Anderson, the proprietor of the razed Bras d'Or House, began to rebuild immediately, and in 1896 the New Bras d'Or House was opened at the same location, across the street from the Telegraph House. The New Bras d'Or House was very different from its predecessor. It had Victorian-era stylings, a covered porch, and a mansard roof, which added another full storey to the building. With sitting rooms on the ground floor, both the second- and third-floor rooms were used for guest accommodations, while the staff occupied the attic.

Anderson proudly advertised the first class accommodations offered by the New Bras d'Or in a 1907 newspaper ad, heralding its "rooms with closets and baths with hot water."

After World War II, the building was remodelled to house a restaurant and apartments.

THE NEW BRAS D'OR
HOUSE, C.1900

JOHN P. MCLEOD AND FAMILY, C.1890

Standing, John P. Sr.; *left to right,* Malcolm, Bella, Christie Ann (Matheson) McLeod, Jessie, Philip, and John P. Jr. (*on his mother's lap*).

John P. McLeod Jr. watched his family's business go up in smoke in 1926, when sparks from the blazing McKay, McAskill, and Company jumped across Main Street to ignite his general store, located on the corner of Cameron and Chebucto streets. He began rebuilding in the same location just days after the disastrous fire that destroyed twenty-six buildings and homes at the east end of Chebucto Street. J. P. McLeod and Sons continued to operate from the cereal mill at the corner of Jones and Chebucto until the new store was ready.

John P. McLeod Sr. was born in Plaister Mines, eight kilometres east of Baddeck, in October 1849. He opened J. P. McLeod's General Store in 1874. Writer Alex McLean described John P. as a "fair dealing and honest man (who) built up a good business." When his three sons, Malcolm, Philip, and John P. Jr., were old enough, they joined him behind the counter and he changed the name of the mercantile to J. P. McLeod and Sons.

John P. Sr. sat on the municipal council for a term from 1890 to 1893, and Philip and John P. Jr. were also elected to the council. Philip won two elections, sending him to the provincial legislature in 1914 and again in 1925. After his father died in 1936, John Jr. moved to Sydney.

An old railway bed is the only reminder of a gypsum quarry that once thrived at the head of Baddeck Bay. The quarry, operated by the Victoria Gypsum Mining Company, was founded by William F. McCurdy (1844–1923), a Baddeck businessman and politician. Established in 1882, the quarry shipped gypsum to customers in Canada and along the eastern seaboard of the United States. Gypsum was quarried at two locations, Red Head and Big Harbour. When a higher quality of rock was found near St. Ann's Bay, a third mine was opened and eventually company headquarters were moved there. At one point McCurdy employed over one hundred men.

Ever the hands-on CEO, McCurdy personally wrote to potential customers, promoting both his product and his location on the Bras d'Or. In an 1887 letter to a customer in Montreal, McCurdy wrote that the gypsum was of a superior quality, available rough or dressed and in a variety of colours:

> We are shipping this season 15,000 tonnes of gypsum rock to one firm in the U.S. They take about 10,000 from one quarry, 5,000 tonnes from another, as rock from one quarry suits for some purposes and [the] other for other purposes. We have deep water for shipping our rock and our harbour is easy of access for vessels of most any size and we have excellent facilities for shipping large quantities. Should you require any quality of rock would it not suit you better to have it shipped from here?

At the end of 1897, operations ceased at the Red Head quarry. In one of his last notations, found near the end of a well-worn ledger book, McCurdy wrote: "I am taking stock, paying my men today and preparing to move."

Another gypsum mine operated briefly at the same location at the head of Baddeck Bay in the 1930s.

SCHOOLCHILDREN AT BADDECK ACADEMY, C.1895

William H. Watson's logo appears on many old photographs, including those of Baddeck Academy students, like this one. His motto advised potential customers of his specialty: "Photographer, Island Scenery, Always on Hand." In 1895, his photos of Baddeck appeared in the American magazine *Outlook*, accompanying an article about Cape Breton.

Based in a small studio near Grant Street, Watson documented life in the village from the mid-1880s until the beginning of the twentieth century. In addition to supplying tintypes and cabinet photographs, Watson also operated a soft drink parlour at the same location, just behind the McKay, McAskill and Company store on Chebucto Street. By 1900 Watson and his family had headed west, leaving scenic views of Baddeck behind for others to capture.

McKay and Company Warehouse at the top of McCurdy's Lane, c.1898

When E. G. McAskill joined McKay and Company in 1903, the store underwent a large renovation, nearly doubling its size. In 1926, a devastating fire that quickly consumed much of Main Street began there.

County clerk Charles McCurdy was the first to notice the fire when an explosion rattled windows, shattering the calm in the early hours of Labour Day Monday, September 6, 1926. McCurdy, who lived across the street from the store, ran to his bedroom window to see smoke pouring from behind the McKay, McAskill building. Charles and his wife, Millie, woke the operator at the central telephone office next door, who in turn began to phone homes to stir sleepy residents. McCurdy then sped to the home of Michael ("Mickle" C.) McLean—caretaker of St. Michael's church, who ran up the hill to the church and rang the bell, alerting the town to the impending disaster. Within minutes, men and women formed a bucket line that began at the courthouse, where a water supply was installed just weeks before.

Explosions continued to rock the McKay, McAskill and Company store sending sprays of flaming kerosene and gasoline over the building, quickly igniting J.P. McLeod's store across the street. As owner Johnny McLeod tried to open the main door of the business built by his father 40 years earlier, he burned his hands on the hot doorknob.

When it was apparent that the fire would take their home too, Charles McCurdy, his wife, and her sister, Winnifred Chase-Brown, left the bucket line to save the contents of their home. Other residents followed and helped them move a treasured roll top desk, a grandfather clock, and

Winnifred's cherished piano across the street and onto the courthouse lawn. Residents scurried to nail wet woolen blankets to the exterior walls of the telephone office while a man atop a ladder soaked the courthouse walls. Such efforts kept the heat and burning embers from igniting the buildings.

McCurdy, meanwhile, left the rescue effort at his own home and rushed into the courthouse to save important county records. Likewise, when the spire of St. Michael's church suddenly ignited, writer Alex McLean and others hurried into the seventy-year-old church to save religious relics. Soon, the bell that first alerted the town to the fire came crashing down.

When a firefighting crew from North Sydney arrived at 5:00 A.M., there was little left to save. In all, the fire destroyed twenty-six homes, businesses, warehouses, and barns at the eastern end of the village.

BADDECK TELEPHONE

Devoted to the Interests of the Farmer, the Merchant and the Tourist. - - - - - Strictly Non-Partisan.

VOL 2.   BADDECK, C. B., JULY 12, 1899.   NO. 25.

ABOVE
DELIVERY BOY, C.1900

TOP OF PAGE
BADDECK TELEPHONE
MASTHEAD, 1899

The *Baddeck Telephone*'s masthead declared that it was "devoted to the interests of the farmer, the merchant and the tourist—strictly non-partisan," but politics brought an end to this vibrant weekly.

The *Baddeck Telephone* was the second newspaper published in Baddeck. Issued from an office at the head of Steamship Wharf (near the present day Baddeck Marine) the six-page broadsheet was chock full of local news. In July 1898, the paper announced: "Dr. and Mrs. Graham Bell, Miss Bell and Miss Marian H. Bell arrived at Beinn Bhreagh last week," and "Mrs. C.B. Fox of Boston is visiting friends at Hunters Mountain and will remain for two months."

The *Telephone* (1898–1900) rose out of the ashes of Arthur McCurdy's *Island Reporter,* the village's first newspaper, which ran from 1884 to 1887. For a decade the *Reporter*'s presses and typeset had remained unused in a waterfront shed until Charles Peppy resurrected the dormant equipment and relocated the paper's headquarters to the west end of Chebucto Street, near Gertrude Hall. (The *Victoria Standard* newspaper was launched in 1991 from the same building.)

The ads in the *Telephone* declared that ladies' sunshades and umbrellas were available for forty cents and up at McKay and Company, and that D. Hutchison, proprietor of Baddeck Marble and Granite Works, was located at the corner of Twining and High streets.

According to writer Alex McLean, an editorial about a long-forgotten political promise to build a bridge across the strait at Little Narrows brought grief to Peppy. The politician sued him for libel and the newspaper folded soon after. It had been published for just over a year.

A decade later, Fred Gilman took over the defunct *Baddeck Telephone* and began publishing the *Victoria News* (1909–1927). Gilman used the same office that Peppy had until he purchased the Hartley Crowdis property (currently the Harvey property) near the old Baddeck Academy on Shore Road. The barn on the property was renovated to hold the print and typeset. From here the *Victoria News* was published until July 13, 1927—the last issue hit the stands the day after Gilman died suddenly.

**HART'S STORE,
C.1900**

Hart's Store was a mainstay on Chebucto Street for more than a quarter of a century. Located on the southeast corner of Chebucto and Prince streets, the mercantile store was built by Joseph Hart, who had moved to Baddeck in 1863 from Margaree. His sons, Charles (1846–1912) and Albert (1858–1940), took over operation of the general store in the mid-1880s. By the turn of the century, Charles had opened a store in Whycocomagh, and Albert was running the operation in Baddeck. When construction began on the Sydney Steel plant in the late 1890s, Albert opened a branch store in Whitney Pier, Sydney.

In a 1940 newspaper article written just months before his death, Albert Hart, then eighty-one years old, recalled being lost in a blinding snowstorm in April 1895. He was leading a team of thirty-two local men with horses and sleighs to Alba, twenty kilometres west of Baddeck, to get loads of hay. Three of the men were his employees, the rest were men recruited from the general area. The trip began uneventfully, but a driving hailstorm halted the returning crew after just a few kilometres. They found two homeowners who agreed to put the men and horses up for the night.

"As we had both supper and breakfast," recalled Hart, "I persuaded Mrs. MacDonald to accept a settlement, but Mrs. Ross would take nothing...all I could do was later to send her a nice young jersey heifer...she was delighted."

In the morning, the storm had passed, but it was too hazardous to travel over the ice with half-tons of hay on each sleigh, so most of it was left behind. The trip back to Baddeck over the frozen lake was arduous, and the men had to stop frequently to shovel a route through the snowdrifts. At six o'clock, after thirty-six long hours, they returned to Baddeck. As Hart prepared to pay the men he was told that they had decided to waive their fees, since he lost money on the venture.

"That is how it was settled. They were good neighbours," he recalled.

CHARLES LEAVER JONES, c.1880

Charles Leaver Jones (1845–1886) was the son of Catherine (Anderson) and William Jones Jr. He was a partner in Jones, Leaver and Company with his brother John and their cousin Leaver Sparling. The shipping company had a waterfront warehouse in the nineteenth century. In the twenty-first century, Jones Street extends north from the company's former location near the present day wharf.

MAIN STREET OF BADDECK AT THE CORNER OF CHEBUCTO AND JONES STREETS, C.1900

In 1900, Robert Elmsley listed over eighty merchants that operated in Baddeck over a forty-year period. While many businesses from that time may be long forgotten today, they were once part of a thriving village. Old newspaper ads provided information about the following establishments.

In 1880, Charles Campbell advertised hardware, boots and shoes, patent medicines, and stationery at greatly reduced prices in exchange for produce. His merchandise, including an August special on one hundred barrels of Bras d'Or herring, was located at the Duntulum warehouse.

In 1899, blacksmith Malcolm Matheson advertised his shop, located at the head of Campbell's wharf as the "headquarters for horseshoeing." That same year, M. K. McGregor detailed his work as a carriage builder and repairer, and as a house and sign painter, at his location on Prince Street.

David Hutchison designed granite and marble monuments at his business, at the corner of Twinning and High streets. In 1900, P. L. MacFarlane, a building contractor, advertised that he manufactured stairs and newels, balusters and doors, sashes, frames, and blinds at his shop at the corner of Prince and Mechanic streets.

R. T. Vooght, who was part owner of a large three-storey department store in North Sydney, opened a branch office in Baddeck in the late nineteenth century. Martin Leist, a German immigrant, was a well-known watchmaker and clock repairer with a shop on the main street near the present-day drug store, and Madame Penelope (Mrs. Metzler Foyle) was well-known for the fortunes she told from her Water Street home.

In 1909, Beinn Bhreagh employees Miss Sarah MacDonald and Miss Annie MacDonald and their escorts Jack MacIvor and Murdoch MacDonald visited Miss Campbell's Ice Cream parlour. In the 1930s Durant and Star cars were advertised as the "best small car on the market" at Bethune's Garage on Chebucto Street.

CHEBUCTO STREET, 1908

This rare photo was found tucked in an album compiled by Baddeck entrepreneur Norman Bethune Sr. (1899–1986). On the back he noted that the man on the right is lawyer Percy Blanchard. Blanchard's law office was located to the right of McKay, McAskill and Company, the large three-storey building.

In the 1940s Baddeck historian Alex McLean wrote about life in Victoria County in a series of unpublished manuscripts. He vividly described the sights of the village's dusty main street lined with horse and buggies, and the sound of old-fashioned leather boots clip-clopping on a wooden boardwalk. In one article, he described the landscape of Chebucto Street prior to the devastating September 1926 fire that wiped out twenty-six homes and businesses.

The McKay, McAskill and Company building was originally built and operated by David McCurdy and his sons, McLean wrote. Around 1888, the business was taken over by Kenneth J. McKay. By 1903, McKay and his brother-in-law, Ewen G. McAskill, had partnered to build a modern mercantile with spacious warehouses. The department store boasted a number of conveniences, including a freight elevator to move unwieldy items up to the third-floor storehouse and down again, and a steam-powered electric lighting plant. It was here that the 1926 fire began.

Beside the department store was the McKay, McAskill warehouse, which housed the stock of heating stoves on the lower floor, and coffins on the upper floor. McLean found the pairing of particular note, writing that there is "often a remote connection between coffins and heat."

Next to the store was the residence of Donald J. McRae, son-in-law of Reverend Alexander Farquharson, a pioneering minister from Middle River. McLean described McRae as a liquor seller who displayed no shame in his profession, despite the temperance of the times: "He handled good liquors and sold them in a manner with an eye to the fitness of things." After the fire, county clerk Charles McCurdy built a home on the site.

Further in the distance is McLeod's General Store, nicknamed Ballachy's, which was owned by brothers Dan and Willie McLeod. By the mid-twentieth century, this had become the location of Stone's Drug Store.

Janet Kidston (at right), granddaughter of early Baddeck settlers William and Margaret Ann, at work in the millinery shop at the McKay, McAskill and Company store. The woman at left is unidentified.

An ad in the September 1898 *Baddeck Telephone* newspaper proclaimed that the store had the largest assortment of goods in the county:

> OUR STOCK of dry goods is complete. In dress goods we keep Priestly's celebrated fabrics in serges, cashmeres and coloured goods with trimmings to suit

> ALSO…flannelette's, prints, greys and white cottons, sheetings, pillow cottons, shirting denims, white and blue dress duck, cottonades, cretonnes, muslins, linens, napkins and towels

> OUR MILLINERY DEPT is in charge of Miss Laura McRae

> JUST RECEIVED a complete assortment of the celebrated "D&A" corsets

> We sell the well known Sibley scythe, the best in the market.

Hartley Crowdis (1865–1938) was a one-man industry. On census records, he is described simply as a "meat-cutter," but this village butcher was an entrepreneurial dynamo. He bought beef "on the hoof" and brought the cattle to his own slaughterhouse just outside of town. Using his own horse-drawn delivery wagon, his cuts of beef were delivered to customers in and around Baddeck.

THE CROWDIS PROPERTY, WITH BADDECK ACADEMY ON THE RIGHT, C.1908

The home he built in 1905, near the corner of Twining Street and Shore Road, was the epicentre of his operation. The dining room was soon converted into an office for bookkeeper Charles Hart. A barber's chair, complete with a standby barber, was installed at the opposite end of the room for Mr. Crowdis and his many employees to get a shave and a haircut at a moment's notice.

In 1980, Haywood's daughter, Nellie, described the many businesses that operated from the property at the turn of the twentieth century:

> He had mail routes, he supplied meat to the [steam] boats and at that time there was no laundry in Baddeck so he had the agency and sent laundry by boat to Sydney....He had the old house [pre-1905] moved down below the meat house and converted into a laundry and then he installed a Chinese man named Tom to run the laundry and live upstairs above it. Where he got Tom I have no idea...I was upstairs in the laundry one day and Tom was sprinkling the clothes."

In addition to the butcher business and laundry, Crowdis delivered mail, owned heavy moving equipment, and operated a blacksmith shop. A Scottish gardener was hired to tend to the garden that bloomed between the house and the Baddeck Academy grounds.

"There was a fruit orchard between the house and the road that went down to the water. My stepmother had a parrot that was always in a case in front of the window. It was a very busy property."

When Haywood Crowdis left Baddeck for California in 1910, he sold the property to Fred Gilman, who published the *Victoria News*, a weekly newspaper, from the large barn at the left of the photo.

WORKERS AT BEINN
BHREAGH LABORATORY;
LEFT TO RIGHT,
JOHN M. McNEIL,
HECTOR P. McNEIL,
RODDIE BETHUNE,
c.1908

Alexander Graham Bell had a modern management style. Over a twenty-year period, his Beinn Bhreagh laboratory employed as many as thirty men and women at a time. These local carriage makers, boat builders, seamstresses, and machinists found themselves working in new industries, often on the cutting edge of technology.

While most of the employees did not have a scientific background, Bell recognized their valuable technical expertise. Dozens of seamstresses were hired to sew red silk onto individual eight-inch tetrahedral cells, which were eventually used in hundreds of kites. Red silk was preferred, as it was a strong material and its dark colour photographed well against the sky. Hector McNeil created metal fasteners to connect the four-sided tetrahedral cells together and shared in Bell's tetrahedral patents.

As an employer, Bell was often generous—he helped one employee pay for a house—but he could also be temperamental. He fired the entire lab staff when they failed to show up during a hurricane. The eccentric inventor apologized the next day and rehired the men. He explained that he had been upset that a windy kite-testing day had been lost.

THE WHITE STORE,
c.1910

D. F. (Donald) McRae knew from the look in Murdoch McDermid's eyes that he would be good for the White Store. Little Murdoch, son of Big Murdoch, had come into the three-storey department store to look for work after school.

So D. F. put the lad to work. Little Murdoch's main chore was to climb a ladder to clean each of the dozens of oil lamps that hung from the high tin ceilings. The job entailed clipping the wicks, cleaning excess oil, and rubbing the glass shades until they gleamed. He would sweep the shiny hardwood floors from the substantial double doors at the front of the store to the back, and the grand staircase up to the second floor. It wasn't long before Murdoch assumed other duties.

By the time D. F. retired and his son George took over, Murdoch was the tailor, taking detailed measurements to create well-fitting suits. When George died in April 1938, Murdoch, who had been there almost as long as the store itself, bought the landmark building.

The White Store originally had three storeys, but according to local folklore, the top floor was removed because it shook in the wind.

By the mid-1950s the store was selling imported women's sweater sets (in pastel shades), mohair blankets, tartans direct from Scotland, fine bone china, and thick Waterford crystal glasses. Much of the upscale merchandise was due to the influence of Murdoch's daughter, Nancy, who had left a teaching career to join her father in running the store in 1954.

The landing of the grand staircase featured photographs of Baddeck, taken in the early days of the twentieth century from the vantage provided by the then-three-storey-high, flat-roofed White Store. The eye-catching window displays often heralded a change in season or holidays, including Easter, Dominion Day, Armistice Day, and Christmas.

Just before Christmas 1973, a blaze destroyed the majestic White Store.

"The treasure it was and the treasures it held, old and new, went to dust," wrote Nancy (McDermid) Langley in 2005.

During World War I, when many members of the Beinn Bhreagh laboratory staff signed up to serve overseas, Alexander Graham Bell hired local women to build rowboats for the British navy.

Gladys (McKinnon) McRae, daughter of Reverend John McKinnon, told an interviewer in the 1980s that she had wanted to see the women working in what was traditionally a male occupation: "I longed to see them at work but I never did. Being brought up by a father (a really good carpenter in spite of two degrees in Theology!) who cringed if he saw a woman try to drive a nail. I wanted to be enlightened to the fact that those girls could really do it!"

In 1926, Walter Pinaud, master boat builder and accomplished sailor, began crafting highly prized yachts at his Baddeck boatyard, re-establishing Baddeck's shipbuilding industry, which had been dormant for forty years.

Pinaud (1885–1968) was born in Prince Edward Island, the son of Martin, a French immigrant who built an impressive reputation as a master craftsman in Charlottetown. Walter learned the age-old skills of boat building from his father.

As he grew, he became a skilled yachtsman, and studied the waves to understand the mechanics of building a sleek boat. He trained further at the Lawley Yard in Boston, an established Massachusetts shipbuilder that constructed state-of-the-art vessels coveted by many yacht captains. He returned to Cape Breton in 1906 to establish his own boatyard in Westmount, a community across the harbour from Sydney.

In 1913, he was hired by Alexander Graham Bell to manage boat building at Beinn Bhreagh. There, he crafted *Elsie,* a sleek fifty-five-foot yawl, designed using Bell's calculations of wave and wind measurements of the Bras d'Or. He was also on hand to construct *Jap,* a speedy trophy-winning motorboat, and the record-setting *Typhoon,* a forty-five-foot ketch that sailed from Baddeck to Cowes, England, in fifteen days in 1920. His own boatyard on a small cove at the western end of the village meant he passed on the family tradition: Pinaud taught his sons Ralph and Fred to craft top quality yachts using Nova Scotia oak and imported mahogany.

An article in the *Berwick Register* in 1956 described the skilled workforce found at Pinaud's boatyard:

> As in the case of most boat building firms in Nova Scotia where craftsmanship is a 'must,' there is little shifting in employment. The firm's key men have been in the yard for years. There is 78-year-old Rod MacLeod for instance. 'He's still going strong as a general ship's carpenter, and I'd hate to have to follow him,' Ralph Pinaud observed. He had the same thing to say for Maurice Watson, another veteran employee who has contributed his part in the maintenance of the yard's high quality of workmanship.

BETHUNE'S GARAGE, 1928

On this sunny Sunday afternoon in June 1928, garage owner Norman Bethune chats with C. A. Fownes, sitting in his 1927 Buick, while Donald Smith smiles from his Studebaker.

Like many of his contemporaries, Norman Bethune went to work at the Beinn Bhreagh labs during the early part of the last century. But this future entrepreneur was restless. He left the Bell labs in 1920 for the Sydney Steel plant. After two years, he was ready to strike out on his own, thanks in part to two plant managers (Mr. Crosson and Mr. Merrill) who backed the mechanic in his plan to open a full-service garage, one of the earliest in the county in 1923. The names of the managers might have been forgotten if not for Bethune's third son, Crosson Merrill, who was named to honour the men.

By 1927, just four years after opening, a new enlarged brick building with three garage bays and a substantial warehouse was built on the same location. The building was eventually expanded into a large five-bay garage with the capacity to hold a dozen cars. At one time eighteen men worked at Bethune's Garage.

Over the next sixty years, Bethune launched a series of enterprises, including a sawmill, an electrical plant that powered the town, and three car dealerships (Star Car, Ford, and GM). In the 1940s his school buses delivered students to schools and home again throughout Victoria County. Just before he retired in the 1980s Imperial Oil Esso awarded him a rare sixty-year pin to mark his years as a gasoline retailer.

HOTEL BADDECK, BADDECK, N.S.

DUNTULUM COTTAGE/
HOTEL BADDECK,
C.1930

Duntulum Cottage was built around 1844 for Baddeck entrepreneur Charles J. Campbell (1819–1906). The grand home was located on the northeast corner of Jones and Chebucto streets, high on a hill overlooking the busy waterfront. Campbell named it Duntulum as a reminder of his ancestral home in Scotland. While on an official visit to Baddeck in 1879, Canadian Governor General Sir John Douglas Sutherland Campbell stayed at Duntulum. Charles proudly wore his Campbell of Bradalbane tartan, a blue-green mix with a vibrant yellow stripe, during the celebrations that went deep into the night. A piper, also outfitted in Campbell tartan, was positioned at the door and instructed to play until the party broke up.

From Duntulum, Campbell watched as the new post office and customs house took shape on the opposite corner of Jones and Chebucto streets in 1885. It was through his political influence as a Member of Parliament that the federal building was constructed in Baddeck. He tinkered with the design, even adding an image of himself as a Scottish chieftain on the keystone above the main door.

After the death of Charles Campbell in 1906, the tradition of hosting politicians at Duntulum continued when William F. McCurdy (1844–1923), one-time provincial politician, made it his home. The house became the Hotel Baddeck in the 1920s when local businessman James Francis Fraser (1873–1958) bought the property.

Fraser was a customs collector and justice of the peace for Victoria County. He was the son of Reverend John Andrew Fraser and Frances Helen Plant, a sister to Robert Elmsley's wife, Mary Ann. James married Frances Haliburton in 1900.

The Hotel Baddeck was described in a 1934 brochure as having "an exceptionally quiet location" with "a number of rooms with private baths" and access to a tennis court. The building burned down in 1967.

A simple stone wall, built during Campbell's time and still located near the sidewalk, is a reminder of the once-grand property of Duntulum Cottage.

FIRST GRADE

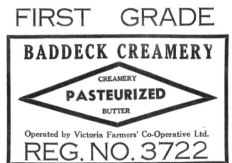

BADDECK CREAMERY

CREAMERY
PASTEURIZED
BUTTER

Operated by Victoria Farmers' Co-Operative Ltd.

REG. NO. 3722

ABOVE

BADDECK CREAMERY BUTTER WRAPPER, c.1950

TOP OF PAGE

BADDECK CEREAL MILL, c.1920

For Anna MacAulay, the Baddeck Creamery was a lifeline. By supplying the government-owned creamery with milk products, the mother of five from Baddeck Bay was able to keep the family's dairy farm operating after her husband, Murdock, died suddenly in 1929. During an interview in 2008, her son Gordon MacAulay Sr. recalled that their fifteen dairy cows provided the family with income through the 1930s: "My mother would get a cheque for thirty-eight dollars a month for the cream she supplied. That was a good income for her."

Anna MacAulay was one of many local farmers to benefit further from the creation of the Victoria Farmers Co-operative in the summer of 1934. The single retail location near the government wharf meant one-stop shopping for customers. Soon afterwards, the co-op bought the government-owned creamery, and in 1940, the co-operative purchased the Nova Scotia Cereal Mill, located on the southwest corner of Jones and Chebucto streets, and converted it into a grocery store.

A fire in December 1946 destroyed the mill building. Within a year, a new store was built at the same location, and it was the site of the co-op for the next forty years. In 1989, a larger, modern building was constructed on Twining Street. Since then, the former co-op building has hosted wedding dances, quilt expos, bingo games, and community meetings as the Baddeck Community Centre.

MACAULAY'S GARAGE, 1948

The days following World War II were a good time to get into business. As servicemen returned home, and buying restrictions on metal and engine parts were lifted, economic prosperity returned to small towns like Baddeck. At one time there were six full-service garages in the village of Baddeck, including Bethune's, John "Mickle" MacLean's, MacFarlane's, Fraser's, MacAulay's, and Phillip's.

While on his honeymoon in 1948, MacAulay visited Ford officials in Saint John, New Brunswick, and began negotiations to bring another Ford dealership to town. When MacAulay and his bride, Ruth (Baker), returned to Baddeck that spring, work began on constructing a three-bay garage on Shore Road, next to Baddeck Academy.

"That [1949] was the first full year we were in operation and we sold sixty units that year. It grew from that. One year we sold five hundred units, but it averaged about three hundred or four hundred," he said in a recent interview, adding that a brand new half-ton truck retailed for about nine hundred dollars at the time.

From his base at the garage, MacAulay was involved in a number of other businesses—he owned shares in the mail boat *Shenacadie*, owned an apartment building, and opened another garage near the Trans-Canada Highway. His businesses employed about thirty people.

"Baddeck is very quiet now, compared with fifty or sixty years ago," MacAulay recalled. "Every Saturday night, farmers from all over came to town and the place would just be filled with people. That's all gone now, completely. It's a very quiet town now."

The opening of the Bell Museum ushered in a new era in the history of Baddeck. The museum, dedicated to the village's most famous resident, provided an opportunity for visitors to learn about Alexander Graham Bell's life and work.

When Bell died in 1922, he left hundreds of artifacts packed to the rafters in the old Kite House on the Beinn Bhreagh Estate. In the 1950s his daughters, Elsie Grosvenor and Marian (Daisy) Fairchild, had the items catalogued and donated to the Canadian government. Their wish was to see the historic material housed in a museum in Baddeck, where Bell had found both solace and inspiration.

On a hot summer day, seventy years after the family arrived in Baddeck, Bell's daughters cut the ribbon to officially open the Alexander Graham Bell National Historic Site. Henry Hicks (the premier of Nova Scotia), J. A. D. McCurdy (the nation's first pilot and then lieutenant-governor of Nova Scotia), and hundreds of local residents attended the opening ceremony. There was an aerial flyby, official ribbon cutting, and strawberry vinegar, Alexander Graham Bell's favourite cooling drink.

The A-frame museum building, designed by O. H. Leicester, incorporated aspects of Bell's tetrahedral structures, with a sweeping triangular roof over the front foyer, which resembles a delta kite in flight.

In 1978, the site expanded to include the original HD-4 and a full-scale model of the hydrofoil boat that established a world speed record in 1919, travelling at 113 kilometres per hour on Bras d'Or Lake.

The museum continues to be a vital part of the Cape Breton economy, not only as a tourism icon that attracts tens of thousands of visitors each year, but as an employer of twenty-five residents—about the same number that once worked across the bay at Bell's Beinn Bhreagh laboratory.

CHEBUCTO STREET, 1958

During the summer of 1958, committees were making plans to mark the fiftieth anniversary of the flight of the Silver Dart in February 1959. The western end of Baddeck still featured many of the main street edifices that existed in 1909.

The iconic White Store was in its twentieth year of operation under Murdock McDermid. The store's large display windows showcased pictures of pilot J. A. D. McCurdy and Mr. and Mrs. Bell, surrounded by flowers (mauve and white phlox, appropriately named "sweet rocket") from the garden of McDermid's wife, Catherine.

In between the White Store and the New Bras d'Or House, then in its sixth decade, was a restaurant operated by Alton Langille, a World War II veteran and POW. He became the new postmaster at the town's modern post office, located at the northwest corner of Chebucto and Queen streets.

Across the street from the post office stood a new kid on the block—Stone's Drug Store. Owner-pharmacist Lloyd Stone established the drugstore in 1954 in the building where McLeod's "Ballachy's" General Store once operated. Before then, prescriptions ordered by Dr. C. L. MacMillan were mailed to Baddeck from Sydney. In the early 1960s Stone, who was inspired to fly after the 1959 Silver Dart anniversary celebrations, occasionally delivered some desperately needed prescriptions to remote patients by dropping them from his plane.

Chapter 2

Transportation and Communication

MARION, C.1895

I t was from this twenty-two-foot side-paddlewheeler that Alexander
Graham Bell, his wife, Mabel, and their two young daughters first
saw Baddeck. The boat's power depended very much on how fast the
stoker, the man in charge of the boilers, could shovel coal.

   This majestic boat made regular trips from Baddeck to Iona,
Whycocomagh, and the Sydneys. Used often in the summer months, it
provided a getaway for picnickers. Members of the Young Ladies Club of

Baddeck took day-long flower-picking excursions, returning home with baskets laden with colourful blooms and small loose bouquets tucked into their hats.

Robert Elmsley, an early postmaster and chronicler, noted the earliest arrival of a steamer when in May 1855, he recorded the *Banshee* rounding the point of Red Head and steaming into Baddeck Harbour. The *Banshee* was said to be the first steam-powered paddleboat built on Cape Breton Island. Constructed in 1851 at Big Bras d'Or, it had a galvanized hull and was built to ferry passengers from communities at North Sydney across the harbour to Sydney. It was soon transferred to the lake run.

The *Marion* was built in New York City in 1876. The ship was 43 metres (142 feet) long, with a tonnage of 478. On October 30, 1922, while the vessel was docked at Whycocomagh, a fire broke out on board. After several failed attempts to contain the fire, the majestic boat was cut from its mooring and set adrift. Its final lake run ended ninety metres from the wharf, where it ran aground and burned. The hull of the ship remained visible in Whycocomagh Harbour for decades afterward.

Angus Tupper's death had a profound effect on the history of Baddeck.

The Onslow, Nova Scotia, farmer-turned-businessman arrived in the village in 1860 to take over one of William Kidston's stores. It was Angus's death five years later that brought the industrious McCurdy family to town. His widow, Hannah (McCurdy) Tupper, summoned her father and brothers to the village to operate Angus's business.

David McCurdy, a future Member of Parliament and a legislator with the province, arrived in Baddeck with three of his five grown sons. The family launched a series of Victoria County businesses, including stores and gypsum mines.

David's son Edward (1842–1927) ran his late brother-in-law's store and was a registrar of probate for Victoria County. Son William (1844–1923) expanded the D. McCurdy and Sons enterprise—a three-storey general store on Chebucto Street (and the eventual location of the McKay, McAskill Store)—building a wharf, a tannery, and establishing the *Island Reporter*, the village's first newspaper. William spotted Alexander Graham Bell's speaking telephone on display at the Philadelphia Exposition in 1876 and immediately grasped its potential. By 1884, he was using the first phones in the village—connecting the waterfront newspaper office with the main street store and his father's home.

Arthur (1856–1923), McCurdy's youngest son (and the father of pilot J. A. D. McCurdy), was working in the newspaper office in September 1885, when according to folklore, Alexander Graham Bell witnessed him fussing with a broken telephone. The inventor entered the office and offered to help fix the apparatus, beginning a lifelong friendship between the Bell and McCurdy families.

MAY QUEEN, C.1897

This little steamer, originally christened the *Mayflower*, was an iron-hulled boat built in 1868 by Sir Sanford Fleming, the engineer responsible for the railway route across Canada and the creator of standard time. The boat was used during the construction of the Intercolonial Railway, and later to ferry passengers, freight, and mail near Pictou, Nova Scotia.

About 1880, the *Mayflower* arrived in Bras d'Or Lake and was renamed the *May Queen*. The 38-metre- (125-foot-) long, side-paddle steamer could carry up to sixty passengers and made frequent stops in Baddeck, Whycocomagh, Grand Narrows, Little Bras d'Or, and West Bay. In April 1883 Robert Elmsley noted that ice in the lake was preventing the *May Queen* from leaving Baddeck for its destination in Whycocomagh.

The boat came to an unceremonious end when it burned on the shore of Kidston's Island in 1898. The fire was described by Alexander Graham Bell in a letter written in June of that year:

> Two nights ago after leaving the Observatory I saw there was a large fire near Baddeck. We woke Miss (Georgina) McCurdy by telephone and she reported that the steamer May Queen was on fire. The May Queen has been

anchored all spring off Kidston's island near the lighthouse, abandoned. A purchaser was found for her, he was to have put in an appearance yesterday, but the fire has rendered his presence unnecessary. Boys have been camping out in her and picnicking on board. I suppose that through their carelessness she has been burned. Mr. Hoppin set out for the burning wreck and spent the night pouring water over the flames in order, as he said, to prevent the island from catching fire.

Benjamin Hoppin was an associate of Bell's who lived on Water Street and would have had a clear view of the *May Queen* beached at Kidston's Island. This photo was probably snapped in the winter of 1897–1898 by Mr. Hoppin's valet, George Hollifield. He often took photographs recording Baddeck people and scenes; many of them include his dog seen in this photo.

Kidston Lighthouse, the first of two lighthouses to grace the entrance to Baddeck Harbour at the east end of Kidston Island, was built in 1875.

Robert Elmsley did not record the exact date the lighthouse became operational. It appears that it was lit for the first time only shortly before it was extinguished for the winter. Elmsley ends the year 1875 with this short entry: "Kidston Island light lit. D. McRae is keeper and put light out for the season."

In the spring, once the ice on the lake had melted and navigation reopened to shipping, the light was kindled once again. The lightkeeper's job of keeping the beacon illuminated required twice daily rows across Baddeck Harbour—the first was just after daybreak to extinguish it; the second, just before dusk to relight it.

As a young girl in the 1930s, Shirley (Dunlop) Kerr made that trip many times. Her grandfather, Bennington McAskill, was the lightkeeper and lived on the waterfront across from the light. She recalled the thrill of landing at the island as the sun was rising and running up the stairs to the top of the lighthouse to watch her grandfather extinguish the light for the day.

In an 1880 almanac, Kidston Lighthouse was described as having a "fixed red catoptric light" —its continuous steady light was aided by a concave mirror for magnification. It was visible for eleven kilometres. The building was a four-sided wooden structure, the kind commonly found on inland waterways like the Bras d'Or.

A new lighthouse was constructed in the early part of the twentieth century, and the taller successor shared the point with its older companion for a number of years. In the winter of 1921, Casey Baldwin, an associate of Alexander Graham Bell, helped move the old lighthouse across the ice to a new location at Shenacadie.

THE TRAIL TO CAMPBELL'S, BAY ROAD, C.1895

In his journal of everyday occurrences, Robert Elmsley (1823–1903) provided invaluable descriptions of the road that runs along Baddeck Bay and into the village. In 1842, he wrote,

> There was not a house to be seen between Joe Campbell's Cove [near the present Boatyard] and old Hector McLean's house, just east of Knox Church [on the Bay Road], except a small log hut of some 16' by 20' where [Alexander] Taylor's House now stands [just east of the pond at the bottom of the museum driveway]. The right of the last named property was purchased for 10 pounds.

Almost fifteen years later, on October 7, 1856, Elmsley recorded in his diary that the first telegraph dispatch from St. John's arrived in Baddeck. The next day he noted that a dispatch sent to the Newfoundland city was answered in fifteen minutes, a response time considered "instantaneous."

In December 1881, he mentioned that new telegraph poles were put up fifty yards apart. By Christmas Eve, there were seventy-five poles from the courthouse at the centre of Chebucto Street to Mrs. Tom Haliburton's gate about a kilometre past Crescent Grove.

Canadian Aerodrome Company test flight on Baddeck Bay, 1910

Following the historic flight of the Silver Dart in February 1909, J. A. D. McCurdy and Frederick "Casey" Baldwin hoped to translate the success of the country's first flight into an aviation industry based at Baddeck.

Applying their successes from the construction and flights of the Aerial Experiment Association, McCurdy and Baldwin formed the Canadian Aerodrome Company and constructed the Baddeck No. 1 and 2 at the Beinn Bhreagh laboratory. Alexander Graham Bell backed the company, with the expectation that the Canadian government would want to invest in the fledgling industry. Through the summer and fall of 1909, the company conducted trials at Bentick Farm in Big Baddeck. Once the winter ice arrived, the testing moved to Baddeck Bay where the planes and pilots were pushed to their limits.

This photo, a postcard sent to California by William MacDonald, an employee at Beinn Bhreagh, shows Baddeck No. 2 "doing good work at Baddeck Bay." MacDonald also added that the plane "made a record flight of half an hour today. Also made two short flights with a passenger." Alexander Graham Bell noted that, in the days that followed, MacDonald and Major G. S. Maunsell, the director of engineering with the Canadian militia, would both go "for a drome over the ice on Baddeck Bay" as passengers.

In one letter to Lord Earl Grey, then the governor general, Bell proposed that the Canadian Aerodrome Company could construct two aerodromes for the Canadian military for ten thousand dollars. This would "aid a new industry to establish itself upon Canadian soil." While some in the military recognized the potential, the official word was that no funds were available for such an experimental expense. By the summer of 1910, the Canadian Aerodrome Company had folded, and the dreams of a Canadian aviation industry at Baddeck died.

Jap, **1910**   In the spring of 1909 sleek wooden motorboats were all the rage.

"This is a beautiful April day and it is a pleasure to breathe the pure fresh air. The ice is fast disappearing and a perfect craze has set in for motor boats," Alexander Graham Bell wrote, as he listed a group of Beinn Bhreagh workers who planned for motorboats of their own. "There will hardly be a row boat left in Baddeck and vicinity when the summer comes on," he noted.

That summer, races were organized and businessmen from across Cape Breton tested their streamlined vessels on the Bras d'Or. The races were set for the evening hours, so as not to interfere with the men's day jobs. The competitions began in Baddeck Bay and ended at a marker three kilometres away near Kidston Island.

Jap, a thirty-five-foot mahogany boat owned by Sydney business-men Peter Campbell, Bert MacLeod, and Dr. MacLellan, was launched in July 1909. The Sydney *Daily Post* described the boat as a "flier" and noted that the vessel's 20-horsepower engine clocked a top speed of twenty-four miles per hour during its first trial in Sydney Harbour. This photo, taken by Gordon Bethune in the summer of 1910, shows *Jap* speeding across Baddeck Harbour. Norman Bethune Sr. (Gordon's brother) noted on the photograph that the *Jap* was built specifically to beat another speedy boat, *Piper*, but could not do so.

In the August 1909 edition of the *Beinn Bhreagh Recorder*, Casey Baldwin, an associate of Alexander Graham Bell and an avid sailor, noted that five motorboats from Beinn Bhreagh had entered a race at Baddeck. Three Beinn Bhreagh boats finished, but they failed to beat the top two finishers—*Jap* and *Piper*. In September of that year, the powerful *Piper* was at the Beinn Bhreagh labs, where it was used to test early hydrofoil models and ferry aviators J. A. D. McCurdy and Casey Baldwin to their aerodrome test field at Bentick Farm in Big Baddeck.

The motorboat craze continued during the next summer. Amid all the speeding boats was John Mickle McLean's motorized canoe.

JOHN MICKLE MCLEAN IN HIS MOTORIZED CANOE, 1910

Vital transportation links, these wide-bodied ships were both work-horses and pleasure craft. A page in a 1902 ledger book detailed a typical trip and the cargo carried: the mail, a horse and a cow (prepaid freight, seventy-five cents each), a horse and wagon (a dollar to come from Iona), a box of helmets for the 94th militia regiment, two cases of corsets for the McKay, McAskill Company, a sofa, a piano, and one case of dry goods for Hart's Store.

The ships were people movers too, taking travellers to the Iona train station, Whycocomagh, and Sydney, and bringing visitors from West Bay and North Sydney. During a typical month in 1907, almost five hundred people travelled between Baddeck and Iona aboard just one of the steamships in operation.

The Victoria Steamship Company and the Bras d'Or Steamship Company operated a number of boats including *Blue Hill*, *Marion*, *Neptune*, *May Queen*, and *Magnolia*. The steamer *Blue Hill* offered regular moonlight excursions to tourists in 1906 and was also available for hire. Occasionally Alexander Graham Bell rented the steamer for three hours at a cost of twenty-five dollars. In December 1907, *Blue Hill* entered the history books as the boat that towed Bell's experimental kite, the Cygnet. In 1917 the two steamship companies merged to form the Baddeck Steamship Company.

FOUR-MASTER SHIP DOCKED AT THE WHARF, c.1920

It was once common to see ships like this four-masted vessel docked at the wharf. Little is known about the ship, but the Bras d'Or Yacht Club (built in 1912) and a renovated McKay, McAskill store, as it looked before the 1926 main street fire, are in the background, dating the photo to between 1912 and 1926. By this time, the age of sail was coming to an end.

HD-4 ON BADDECK BAY, 1919

Each time its two 350-horsepower engines roared to life, Baddeck residents knew the HD-4 would soon be speeding past. The engines of the cigar boat, as it was called by many in Baddeck, were without mufflers, so the noise of the boat racing on the bay echoed across the surrounding hillside. Some farmers complained that their cows would run in fear at the noise, then refuse to milk.

The experimental hydrofoil boat pictured here was an eighteen-metre, five-ton vessel designed by Alexander Graham Bell and Casey Baldwin. In September 1919, it established a world speed record of 113 kilometres (70.86 miles) per hour on the Bras d'Or Lake, a record that stood for almost a decade.

Bell and Baldwin's hydrofoil experiments evolved from their work in the Aerial Experiment Association between 1907 and 1909. Their early intentions were to design an aircraft that could take off and land on water, but while in Italy in 1910, Bell and Baldwin witnessed Enrico Forlanini's hydrofoil boat skimming the waves. When they returned to Beinn Bhreagh, they switched from aircraft testing to high-speed boats.

The HD-4 (HD refers to the word "hydrodrome") was the fourth in a series of full-size boats built at the Beinn Bhreagh boatyard between 1911 and 1921. The boatyard designed as many as eight hydrofoil boats, with accompanying small models, but only four full-size versions were constructed. After the United States entered World War I in 1917, Bell and Baldwin hoped to market the vessels as stealthy submarine chasers, but the war was over before they developed a suitable model.

In the 1920s the HD-4 was beached. It remained on the shore at Beinn Bhreagh, where generations of Baddeck kids played on its weathered wood. In the 1970s it was donated to Parks Canada and preserved. Since then it has been on permanent display at the Alexander Graham Bell National Historic Site.

Casey Baldwin's history-making flight in upstate New York during the winter of 1908 can be credited, in part, to his lack of suitable footwear on the ice. As his fellow members of the Aerial Experiment Association skated around the Red Wing at Hammondsport, New York, Casey Baldwin was slipping and sliding in his shoes, so the aviation group decided he should take the pilot's seat. He entered the history books, becoming the first Canadian to fly.

Born in Toronto in 1882, Frederick "Casey" Baldwin was the grandson of Robert Baldwin, a pre-Confederation politician in Ontario. He excelled at sports, baseball in particular, and was nicknamed Casey after the popular poem "Casey at the Bat." At the University of Toronto, he was captain of the cricket team and led the football team to an intercollegiate championship in 1905, winning the game in the dying seconds. He was also a baseball player, golfer, and fencer.

Baldwin arrived in Baddeck in the summer of 1906, a newly minted mechanical engineer. His fresh ideas invigorated Alexander Graham Bell, and within weeks of his arrival, the pair designed a seventy-foot lookout tower for the hill at Beinn Bhreagh. Constructed with tetrahedral cells, the tower was built to prove how strong, yet lightweight, the tetrahedron design could be.

"Father and Mr. Baldwin are wild over steel tetrahedrons," Mabel Bell wrote to her daughter Daisy that summer. "If only I had a third daughter, she should have this young fellow—but he seems to have no thought but tetrahedrons."

An avid sailor, Baldwin was at the helm of the *Typhoon* in 1920 when it sailed from Canada to England in a record-breaking fifteen days. As a member of the provincial legislature for Victoria County (1933–1937), he oversaw the establishment of a national park in the Cape Breton Highlands.

The *O-We-Ra* has a storied and moneyed past. The boat was built in Scotland in 1907 for Frederick Stevens, a New York State senator.

According to a *New York Times* article from that year, the five-hundred-ton steam yacht was capable of maintaining speeds of eighteen knots. The vessel was frequently chartered by Nelson Aldrich, a temperamental senator from Rhode Island and future grandfather to Nelson Aldrich Rockefeller, heir to the Standard Oil fortune and vice-president of the United States following the Watergate scandal in 1974.

In the summer of 1910, Nelson Aldrich took *O-We-Ra* on an unplanned trip to Marblehead, Massachusetts, for an impromptu chat with President Taft. He encountered strong winds along the way. "The *O-We-Ra* bucked a northeast gale off Cape Cod early today that gave all hands a good taste of strenuous North Atlantic weather," the newspaper reported.

A May 1915 social page write-up in the *Times* noted a change in the vessel's ownership: "Mr. and Mrs. (Peter & Mathilde) Gerry made the trip to San Francisco on the *O-We-Ra* going via the Panama Canal." Two years later, when the United States Navy entered World War I, it leased the boat from Gerry, who was then senator for Rhode Island, and used it to patrol the waters off Long Island Sound. When the war ended, the vessel was returned to the Gerrys.

While research has answered some questions about the *O-We-Ra*, others remain. Why did this boat dock at the Baddeck wharf? Who was on board? Why were a Mountie and pipe band on hand?

In December 1898, the *Baddeck Telephone* reported that phone service had come to town: "Baddeck, Little Narrows, Orangedale and Whycocomagh [are] now connected by telephone. We are pleased to note Mrs. E. M. (Emily) Sparling [is] in charge of head office." Sparling, the daughter of postmaster Robert Elmsley, was the second generation of her family to be aware of the community's comings and goings.

ANNA (MCPHAIL) LONG, TELEPHONE OPERATOR, c.1950

The convenient telephone service fit quite easily into everyday life. Three months later, by March 1899, Charles Peppy, the newspaper's editor, wrote: "The wonder now is how it was done without for so long."

Sparling directed the telephone traffic from an office located beside St. Michael's Church until 1911, when Bessie McAskill, the future wife of Gerald Dunlop, took over. The office was relocated to the south side of Chebucto Street, to a site between Charlie McCurdy's (pre-1926) home and the Royal Bank. During the great fire of 1926, as the McCurdy house went up in flames, residents soaked woollen blankets and nailed them to the side of the telephone office. Had it not been for this effort, the office would have been destroyed along with the twenty-six other buildings lost in the fire.

Muriel (Long) Carmichael, ran the office with her husband, Harry, in the 1950s. "I can still see Mrs. Grosvenor [Bell's daughter] yet, coming into the office to make calls. Sometimes she'd have to wait because of the party lines and other times she was waiting for long distance calls," she recalled in 2008. The most popular calls were to the Co-op (number 41) and Bethune's Garage (number 23). Being on a party line meant that "you were never alone. It was nice," Carmichael said.

The switchboard and central office were in operation twenty-four hours a day until 1968 when dial service was installed in Baddeck. Baddeck's telephone agents were: Emily Sparling; Esther Arsenault; Winnie McKay; Fanny MacKay; Fred W. MacDonald, his wife, and son; Mrs. Alex Long, Harry Carmichael, and Mrs. Charles Nicholson.

J. A. D. McCurdy, c.1959

He is best remembered as the pilot of the first heavier-than-air flying machine in Canada, but John Alexander Douglas McCurdy (1886–1961) continued his pioneering ways in the field of aviation as an early barnstormer, world-record holder, and founder of the nation's first flying school.

Born in Baddeck on August 2, 1886, he was the son of Lucy (O'Brien) and Arthur Williams McCurdy. His father helped the Bell family find a house to rent when they decided to make Baddeck their summer home, and he later became Bell's secretary. Arthur McCurdy was an inventor as well, patenting a photography film-developing tank, called the Ebedek (the Mi'kmaq word for Baddeck), which he later sold to Kodak.

After piloting the Silver Dart in February 1909, McCurdy earned his wings as a stunt flyer, developing his own figure-eight manoeuvre as he barnstormed across the United States. He accepted a challenge from a Cuban newspaper to fly 145 kilometres over open water from Key West, Florida, to Havana, a trip never before attempted in an airplane. A watch and thirty-five-cent compass were his only instruments. He set down a few kilometres short of the Cuban shores, but the flight set a distance record.

When World War I began five years later, Canada was still without an air force, but not without pilots. McCurdy's flight school in Toronto, where a potential pilot could receive four hundred minutes of training for four hundred dollars, taught flyers who were qualified to fly with the Royal Flying Corp in Britain.

By 1919, McCurdy's barnstorming days were behind him, but he remained in the aviation industry, running the Curtis-Reid Aircraft Company in Montreal. In 1948, Prime Minister Mackenzie King appointed him the lieutenant-governor of Nova Scotia.

In February 1959, McCurdy, then seventy-two years old, was Canada's oldest living pilot. During the fiftieth anniversary celebrations of the flight of the Silver Dart that year, he was flown to Baddeck by the Royal Canadian Air Force, the branch of the military he envisioned in 1909. His plane landed on the frozen lake where he had entered the history books half a century earlier.

He died in June 1961 and was buried at Knox Cemetery, where his grave overlooks Baddeck Bay.

BADDECK, K147, c.1945

This flower class corvette was commissioned in May 1941, and christened HMCS *Baddeck,* in honour of the village. It was one of seventy corvettes built by the Canadian Navy between 1939 and 1941. Lieutenant Alan Herbert Easton of London, Ontario, was the HMCS *Baddeck's* first commanding officer. He oversaw a crew of eighty-five sailors.

In October 1941 the HMCS *Baddeck* was part of a fifty-two-ship convoy escorting merchant vessels overseas. In addition to conducting patrols, the ship searched the North Atlantic for survivors when nine ships were torpedoed. It also took part in the Allied invasion of Normandy in June 1944.

After the war, the ship was sold to Greece and used as a merchant ship. It sank there in 1947. The only remaining example of the flower class corvette is the HMCS *Sackville*, on permanent display at the Maritime Museum of the Atlantic on the Halifax waterfront.

Each ship had a badge, often a play on the vessel's name, which was posted on the foredeck. The HMCS *Baddeck's* symbol was a hand of cards with five aces—a bad deck.

Seaplane used by the department of lands and forests, c.1959

This seaplane was a frequent visitor to the Baddeck waterfront throughout the 1960s. It was used by the provincial department of lands and forests to scout for forest fires and possible insect outbreaks in the province's Crown land forests in the Highlands.

The plane attracted a small crowd of aviation enthusiasts each time they heard the whine of its engines.

"There was excitement, (because) it didn't happen every day," Baddeck resident Lloyd Stone recalled in a 2008 interview. Stone, a pilot, flew in the seaplane a number of times while assisting forestry personnel on trips to Big Baddeck and Meat Cove.

In this photo, the plane is docked near the Bras d'Or Yacht Club. The homes of Charles McAskill (with clothes on the line), Captain Angus Carmichael, and Janie Nicholson are visible in the background.

Chapter 3

People

JOE MOLLY, 1913

H is name is found on an 1871 census of First Nations people in Cape Breton and, according to local folklore, Joe Molly (1833–1916) was the last full-blooded Mi'kmaq on the island. The thirty-eight-year-old lived in a wigwam in Wagmatcook, ten kilometres west of Baddeck, with his thirty-two-year-old wife, Julieanne, and their daughters, Madelin, two, and Mary, one. He listed his occupations as cooper and fisherman, and stated that he could read English. Molly was also a medicine man, highly respected in the Mi'kmaq culture, who was believed to have unearthly powers to heal the sick, locate game and fish, and forecast the weather.

A postcard sent to the United States from Baddeck provides an eyewitness account of a Mi'kmaq camp along the shores of the Bras d'Or Lake in 1899:

> My dear Clara,
>
> I am at Baddeck now, on the Bras d'Or Lakes. There are several Indian encampments here. They do not live in tents as our Indians do, but they do build wigwams out of birch bark and inside they have little hammocks made out of an old blanket, that is where the little babies sleep. They are very white and do not look like Indians. The Indians are called Micmacs. There is only one full blooded Indian here in Baddeck. He is very old. I took his picture on board the boat coming from Sydney here.

The 1800 wedding of William Jones Sr. and a very pregnant Mary Leaver on a small outcropping of land in the Bras d'Or (now submerged) sounds like the beginning of a good novel. The bride was accompanied by her shotgun-toting brothers, and William Sr. had to be intercepted by a rowboat when he tried to flee. Once married, William succeeded in leaving town and never returned. William Jones Jr. was born just weeks after his parents' hastily arranged marriage.

In a letter dated July 12, 1803, three years after the event, Jonathan Jones, William Sr.'s father, wrote about the delicate situation:

> With respect to William [it's] a female commotion that sent him from home. Tho far from being infamous, she is of a creditable family in moderate circumstances whom he privately married and left her immediately...I was entirely ignorant of the matter till it was too late to interfere for he was gone to Newfoundland....I have not seen him since.

Jones added that if his son was determined not to live with his wife, then his coming home would "only make a bad thing worse."

Of William Jr., his first grandchild, Jones wrote that he was "a remarkable fine boy who we are all as fond of as is possible to be, we have him with us as often as he can be spared from home." When Jonathan Jones died around 1810, he left two hundred acres of land on the Baddeck River to his grandson.

Regardless of the circumstances surrounding his birth, William Jones Jr. seems to have lived a quiet life. He was the second non-native child born in Big Baddeck and the first male. His early education was informal and home-based. At the age of ten, he was living in Main-a-Dieu with his paternal aunt, doing his math sums in the sand on the beach.

William Jr. became a justice of the peace, and as a result his name is found on numerous early court documents, his signature a tight, neat script. He married Catherine Anderson in 1828, and the couple had eight children, including Robert, father of Mary Jones Bethune. In 1832 he was made surveyor of high roads and fence viewer for Baddeck. As late as 1880, the year he died at age seventy-nine, he was listed as a judge of probate and a commissioner of schools for Victoria County.

Lieutenant James Duffus (circa 1795–1833) was a first-generation immigrant to the wilds of Canada. His father, William, was a prosperous Scottish tailor who settled in Halifax in the 1780s. James spent time in the Royal Navy, reportedly aboard HMS *Falcon,* which saw service during the War of 1812. A distinctive scar across his forehead, he was known to say, was the result of a sword-swinging fight on board the ship. In Halifax, Duffus's stepsister married shipping magnate Samuel Cunard. It was he who spied a number of possible business ventures on Cape Breton and encouraged James to explore them.

In October 1818, Duffus married Margaret Ann McDougall in Halifax. Soon afterward, the couple arrived in Cape Breton, finding a few small and newly established communities scattered around the Bras d'Or Lakes at Boularderie, Middle River, and Big Baddeck. James built a home and shop on a sliver of land just off the mainland in St. Patrick's Channel. There were no settlers on the shore opposite him at that time, though the property would eventually become the village of Baddeck. He staked a claim for the small island and some four hundred acres opposite, naming the spit of land Duke of Kent Island. In the 1820s Margaret gave birth to two sons while James was appointed magistrate.

The Duffus store soon prospered. Customers travelled a well-worn footpath eight kilometres from Big Baddeck to the shore opposite Duffus mercantile and waved a white handkerchief to summon a canoe to pick them up from the mainland. The clerk, Charles J. Campbell, would collect the customer from the shore, paddle across the narrow strait, and deposit them on the island to complete their shopping. The service was free.

By 1833, Duffus was in Halifax seeking medical help, and died soon afterward. Margaret was left alone on the island to operate the store.

David Sr. and Catherine (McGrath) Dunlop raised five children (twins James and David Jr., John, Annie, and Maud) in the Telegraph House Hotel, and each child was expected to help with the business.

When David Dunlop Sr. died in May 1885, twins James (1855–1914) and David Jr. (1855–1916) took over the business. In 1887, David married Isabella Taylor, and their son, James Gerald (1891–1954), married Bessie McAskill (1890–1979) in 1918. Gerald and Bessie would continue the tradition of operating the Telegraph House while raising a family within it.

When James Dunlop, the high sheriff of Victoria County, and his new bride, Christine (MacDonald), returned to Baddeck from Boston after they eloped in April 1889, people began to gather on the dock. Flags of every description decked the homes and businesses of the main street. As the steamer *Neptune* approached the wharf, the crowd shouted, "Hip-hip hurrah!" and "There they are!" in honour of the newlyweds.

Later, Alexander Graham Bell, who had also been on board the steamer, bunked at the Telegraph House, but his slumber was disturbed by wedding serenaders: "They blew horns and they drummed on tin cans and they shouted in discord 'For he's a jolly good fellow which nobody can deny.' Three or four parties of serenaders made their appearance and were let into the dining room, where they were regaled on bride's cake and port wine. Then quietness settled down upon the scene and Baddeck became itself again."

In 1914, James's sudden death from a heart attack at age fifty-nine was recorded by Bell in the Home Notes, a diary of everyday happenings. Bell noted the Beinn Bhreagh flag was at half-mast and stores in the village were closed during the funeral.

One of the founding members of the Young Ladies of Baddeck Club and the youngest child of David Catherine, Maud Dunlop (1861–1933) was a force to be reckoned with. Noted authors and famous inventors alike were charmed by her winsome ways. Charles Dudley Warner described her as "the lovely Maud," and she was fondly remembered by Arctic explorer George Rice. Alexander Graham Bell set out to find her when he arrived in Baddeck for the first time.

In 1887, Maud married Baddeck merchant Murdock MacKenzie and the couple had four children. All three of her sons died as a result of their service in World War I. Her daughter, Catherine MacKenzie Bierstadt (1890–1948), was Alexander Graham Bell's secretary for fourteen years and became a published author who penned a history of Bell's life. Bierstadt was also an award-winning editor for the *New York Times*, often writing columns under the pen name Maud Dunlop, her mother's maiden name.

His eye framed some of the earliest views of the Arctic landscape.
George Walter Rice (1855–1884) was the official photographer of the
Lady Franklin Expedition (also known as the Greely Expedition) of
1881–1884.

His parents, Frederick and Mary Ann (Munn) Rice, were farmers
who worked the land near Baddeck Bay. George was listed as a sixteen-
year-old farmer on the 1871 census and was born within weeks of the
Dunlop twins, James and David Jr. His playground was the village's
dusty main street and, of course, the lake, where he learned to sail. It is
unknown when or where George became smitten by the twins' younger
sister, Maud, forever memorialized in Charles Dudley Warner's travelogue as "a flitting sunbeam of a girl," but she remained forever in his
thoughts.

By 1880 the twenty-five-year-old George had attended Columbia
University in New York, been an assistant in his uncle's Washington,
D.C., photography studio, and found himself on an expedition to
Greenland. The next year, he was recruited by the United States Signal
Corp to join the Lady Franklin Expedition. Aldophus Greely, later one
of the founders of the National Geographic Society, led the expedition,
part of an international effort to establish scientific observation stations
around the still-unexplored North Pole.

The Arctic was as foreign as the face of the moon in the late nineteenth century, and George Rice documented the unforgiving landscape at Fort Conger, the base the expedition built on the northern-

most tip of Ellesmere Island. His lively spirit lifted the crew during the near-total darkness of the Arctic winter days.

But the group was doomed when two separate attempts to replenish the camp failed. Following a pre-arranged plan, the twenty-five men trekked four hundred kilometres south, carting thousands of pounds of scientific equipment and supplies over the frozen land and ice-packed waters to Cape Sabine. Rice carefully carried dozens of eight by ten glass plate negatives of his photos.

Once the crew arrived at Cape Sabine, they waited for months for a rescue ship. The men fought against frostbite, starvation, and hypothermia as their food supply dwindled, eventually boiling their sealskin boots for sustenance when it finally ran out. The group considered Rice a hero. He conducted searches of the barren landscape in sub-zero temperatures to seek out food, and he even devised a fishing net that could fit through a slim crack in the ice, scooping up hundreds of tiny, hard-shelled underwater creatures that the men boiled into a crunchy stew. While most of the men were too weak to move, Rice hiked the three kilometres daily to the fishing grounds and back to provide his comrades with this meagre, but vital, nourishment.

Starving, emaciated, and struggling against a fierce April snowstorm while on a search for food, George Rice died of hypothermia. "He was too weak to stand. His mind seemed to be taken up with recollections of his relatives and friends at home...he also kept talking of the different meals he would eat when he should have reached home," Julius Fredericks, his associate, later wrote. Rice was buried in a shallow grave in the frozen North.

Two months later, when a ship finally broke through the ice, only six of the original twenty-five crew members remained alive.

Found among Rice's effects in the North, was a note: "In the event of this pending journey ending fatally for me...Of my trinkets I desire that a diamond ring, which will be found among my effects, to be sent to Miss Maud Dunlop of Baddeck, Cape Breton, as a souvenir of a few sunshiny days." It was likely no coincidence that Maud would later name her youngest son George.

Leaver Sparling's parents brought together two of the earliest Loyalist families to settle in Big Baddeck. His mother, Maria (Leaver), was the granddaughter of Jonathan Jones, and Leaver's father, James Sparling, was a descendent of pioneer settler Peter Sparling. Leaver (1840–1889) and his cousins established Leaver, Jones and Sparling, a mercantile with a warehouse on the Baddeck waterfront.

LEAVER SPARLING, c.1885

In her unpublished manuscript, "Some Early Baddeckers: A genealogy of the Sparlings and Elmsleys," Florence Sparling described Leaver as being short in stature and somewhat of a natty dresser. In June 1885, Sparling married Emily Elmsley, eldest daughter of postmaster Robert Elmsley. The pair tied the knot at Sackville House, the Elmsley home on the Bay Road near the present-day entrance to Bell Bay Golf Course. Florence Sparling quoted a newspaper article, likely the *Island Reporter*, that described the ceremony:

> A brilliant assemblage last night at Sackville House, the residence of Robert Elmsley esq. Postmaster, witnessed the nuptial of Mr. Elmsley's charming daughter Emily M. and Mr. Leaver Sparling, merchant of this town. The ceremony was performed by Rev. Davies in a very impressive manner. The happy couple were congratulated by their many friends after which the groom was initiated into the Right Royal Grand Degree of matrimony by his best man, assisted by several other gentlemen to the great amusement and mystery of the uninvited. Next came a salute with rive and slippers as the happy couple drove off to catch the Neptune by which steamer they left for a bridal tour.

The couple settled in Massachusetts and had a son. Leaver was working as an insurance salesman when he became sick and died of tuberculosis in August 1889. Emily, with one young son and pregnant with another child, returned to Baddeck, where she would eventually become the chief telephone operator.

GARFIELD MACKAY
(SECOND ROW, FAR
RIGHT, AND SHOWN
ABOVE), c.1896

For years, Garfield "Libby" MacKay (1882–1963) was the caretaker of the books at the Baddeck Public Library. She was the typical bespectacled librarian, living a quiet life in a small Nova Scotia town. But her earlier career as a nurse was far from staid. As a member of the Canadian Army Nurse Corps, she was on the front lines in France, tending to battered soldiers and living under constant threat of attack.

When she returned to North America, she worked with the New York Association for Improving the Condition of the Poor as a public health nurse, which took her deep into the slums of Little Italy in New York City. There she taught mothers how to prepare nutritious meals, assisted dentists, and helped families in times of crisis. She wrote a letter to her friends at the Alexander Graham Bell Club in Baddeck describing the experience:

> To me one of the most interesting departments is that called 'family welfare,' the idea being that it's better to support a family entirely through some misfortune and keep them together than to send the children to orphanages and such places and let the mother work. For instance, in a family where the father has tuberculosis and has to have perhaps a years rest and care in a sanitarium, the (N. Y.) A. I. C.P. will take entire care of the family during his absence. For such a case the man has no worrying about the support of the family and the chances for his recovery are increased.

ABOVE

WILLIAM KIDSTON JR. AND SON, C.1867

TOP OF PAGE

VIEW FROM THE BAY ROAD, C.1898

This photo offers a view through the narrow strait between Kidston's Island and Baddeck. James Duffus built his store and residence in this clearing on the island. Few buildings existed on the shore at that time, and none in the vicinity that would become the village. But William Kidston (1814–1882) had a vision that a town would grow from the undeveloped land that lay across from Duffus's island.

When he married Margaret Ann McDougall Duffus (1799–1887) in 1836, Kidston thus became the owner of the four hundred acres of land that was soon known as Baddeck. (At the time, the name belonged to the community eight kilometres to the west. In the earliest days of settlement, the shore across from the island was called Little Baddeck to distinguish it from the older community. Between 1836 and 1860, Little Baddeck outgrew its name and became simply Baddeck.)

Kidston and Margaret Ann continued to live on the island, which was soon renamed in his honour, and their three children—Archibald, Isabella, and William John Jr.—were born there.

Kidston lobbied for a new government separate from Cape Breton County with its seat of power at Baddeck. He donated land at the centre of the new main street for a courthouse. As the architect of the new community, he began to sell lots to businessmen, plotting the main street while there were still only a handful of people living there.

In 1877, William Kidston's nephew, Samuel McKnight, visited him in Baddeck. By then the village was a bustling, well-populated community, and Kidston had moved from the island to Water Street. Of his uncle's home, McKnight wrote: "The house is only a few years old, (and) was built all together by Uncle William's own hands and is rather pretty looking."

If it happened in Baddeck, Robert Elmsley (1823–1903) knew about it. As postmaster and registrar, he had his finger on the pulse of the community. Born in Breechin, Scotland, on October 4, 1823, he immigrated to Cape Breton as a teenager and arrived in Baddeck (he noted specifically) at 3:40 P.M. on March 21, 1840. He worked as a clerk for William Kidston in the first store on what he called "Mutton Island."

Over the course of thirty-four years, Elmsley kept a diary of the comings and goings of business people, their marriages, births, and deaths, any whiff of political scandal, and of course, the weather.

Elmsley's diary began simply on December 30, 1855: "Steamship *Banshee* came to her wharf at Baddeck with goods and 30 passengers." His day-to-day jottings provide some of the earliest and best descriptions of everyday life before the Bell family arrived in Baddeck in 1885.

"There were no roads at this time," he recalled of his earliest days in Baddeck. "The sea beach was used from Charles Campbell's store to Hector McLean's log house east of Knox Church and probably a track was blazed though the woods north for those who had no boat."

In his sometimes maddeningly brief entries, he noted the historic (the first telegraph message received from St. John's, Newfoundland, in October 1856), the ordinary ("Fine day," on September 9, 1871), and the unusual (a running tab on the weight of his wife, their children, and notable residents).

His own life was also fully on display: his single entry for the month of June 1856 said "Robert Elmsley married at bar (North Sydney) to Miss M. A. Plant." He also noted, in typical new-parent mode, the milestones of his six-week-old, first-born daughter: "November 15, 1859, Emily went out, first time."

Elmsley wrote his final entry in March 1889. When he died in 1903, he had lived in Baddeck for more than half a century. Arriving when there were only a handful of homes scattered along the shoreline, he walked in the same footsteps as the village pioneers, witnessed the largest growth the village ever experienced, and left a priceless record for future generations.

CHRISTINA TAYLOR (SEATED) AND HELEN TAYLOR AT THEIR HOME ON SHORE ROAD, C.1900

Christina Taylor (1825–1910) and her husband, Alex Taylor Sr., were among the earliest settlers to the village of Baddeck, building a house on the Bay Road near the pond. As early as January 18, 1857, postmaster Robert Elmsley noted that he had taken tea at the Taylors' home.

According to Elmsley, the Taylors had the first wagon able to ride the rough footpaths that would become the town's roads, so Mrs. Taylor was known as one of the first people to use a wheeled vehicle in Baddeck. After the death of her husband in October 1887, Christina moved in with her son, Alex Jr., his wife Helen (Munro), and their two daughters, Emily and Janie.

Helen (1855–1908) was born in Boularderie. She was the daughter of Alexander and Catherine Munro, early educational innovators who built their own school in Boularderie. Helen and daughter Emily were founding members of the Young Ladies Club of Baddeck in 1891.

Thirteen-year-old Janie Taylor was the youngest invitee to The Lodge at Beinn Bhreagh on October 10, 1891.

The town's women had been asked to Mrs. Bell's home to form an educational and social club. Janie, who came with her mother, was closer in age to Mrs. Bell's two daughters and niece, who were not part of the excited group and peeked out from behind a curtain to watch the proceedings. During the meeting, the group approved a constitution and voted in a slate of officers. Janie was surrounded by formidable women like Mabel Bell and Georgina McCurdy, yet she was selected as first secretary of the Young Ladies Club of Baddeck.

The secretary's job was to record the minutes of the meetings, noting motions and seconders, take notes about the presentation that followed, conduct roll call of the members, and collect dues. "I was just a little girl and very unqualified for the position and until I became more efficient I used to go to Miss (Georgina) McCurdy (club president) every week and have her help me with the minutes," Taylor recalled in 1928.

When Mrs. Bell started a sewing school for girls in Baddeck, she likely noted young Janie's maturity. Janie and her sister, Emily, attended the school, and it was there the girls first learned plain sewing, then delicate embroidery. "When we became expert enough we were paid for any work we did. I know several girls who were able…to add considerably to their pin money by doing work of this kind," Janie wrote in 1923.

In 1904, when the girls had become young women, Alexander Graham Bell noted in a letter to his wife that a work exchange was in place at Gertrude Hall, where local sewers and weavers displayed their handcrafted wares: "Between July 20th and August 20th, Miss Taylor has sold articles to the amount of $20.40…The visitors at the hotels also are learning about the Exchange—and visit Gertrude Hall to look over the collection."

As the wife of a country doctor, Mary Catherine Jones Bethune (1866–1955) had unusual housekeeping challenges—her home had a surgery room where she was often called upon to assist her husband.

Mary was the only child of Janet (Cameron) and Robert Jones, and was a great-great-granddaughter of Jonathan Jones, the first permanent settler in the area. Before she was a year old, her father died of tuberculosis. For income, her mother began to rent rooms in their home to boarders. In 1875, shortly after graduating from Dalhousie University in Halifax, Dr. John Lemuel Bethune arrived in Baddeck. The native of Loch Lomond, Richmond County, planned to buy a house near the waterfront and set up a practice. But his plans were dashed when the house he planned to buy burned. He found temporary lodgings at the Jones house, where ten-year-old Mary, a studious and introspective girl, was already enrolled in high school. (When Mary began school in the early 1870s, it was in a small one-room building near the Baddeck waterfront.)

At sixteen she was teaching at the new Baddeck Academy, a two-storey schoolhouse on Shore Road. A romance developed between the dashing doctor and the thoughtful teacher, and the pair married in January 1885 on Mary's nineteenth birthday. In later years, Mary joked that for her honeymoon she simply walked across the hall.

The couple had seven children, six sons and a daughter, losing toddlers, Douglas, two, and Maxwell, one, in a diphtheria outbreak in 1899. Mary's sons' playmates were the McCurdy boys—Douglas (J. A. D.), George, and Lucien—who lived just up the road. (In fact, it was during a birthday party in her backyard that young Douglas—the future pilot of the Silver Dart—exploded a cap of gunpowder, nearly severing his hand.) When Mary's husband died suddenly in 1913, her youngest child was just seven years old. She took a position as registrar of deeds, a job once filled by her father.

As a founding member of the Young Ladies Club of Baddeck (later the Alexander Graham Bell Club), she helped to write programs and present them, often providing detailed accounts to the Baddeck and North Sydney newspapers.

Georgina McCurdy (1840–1928) was almost fifty years old when her youngest brother, Arthur, was left a widower after his wife, Lucy, died days after giving birth to the couple's fourth child. In the days and months that followed, Georgina stepped in and became mother to Arthur's four children—George, Susan, Douglas, and Lucien.

When Arthur became Alexander Graham Bell's secretary and moved to Washington, D.C., for the winter of 1894, there were plans for the Bell family to adopt Douglas, the future pioneering pilot—that is, until Aunt Georgie, who felt the family should be raised together, had her say. Young Douglas did live in the United States with the Bell family that winter, but the adoption plans were nixed.

Susan, Georgina's niece, recalled in 1928 that her aunt's style of parenting was very progressive for the time:

> I was too young to appreciate how splendidly she was bringing the children up, but I do remember distinctly that her method of handling them was always a keen delight to my father. It fitted in with all his theories and he would chuckle over the clever way she managed that any punishment should be the natural consequence of what they had done that was naughty, and not something that she was arbitrarily inflicting on them.

Georgina was elected first president of the Young Ladies Club of Baddeck at the first meeting in October 1891, and she was also elected to sit on the first board of governors. "I was inwardly scared to death to be chosen as the head of a new and untried organization, though outwardly I may have appeared unruffled," she recalled in 1924.

Mabel Bell paid tribute to Georgina in 1905:

> The life and soul of everything, a devoted daughter to her father, a beautiful mother to her brother's children, a wise president of our club, a hard working woman and yet, what one thinks most of about her is her youth, courage and joyousness, she enjoyed everything so much. I am sure nobody ever was with her half an hour without feeling happier and sure that things weren't so bad after all.

CHARLES MACASKILL, MAY 1908

In this photo, undertaker Charles MacAskill (1860–1950) stands at the front of a horse-drawn hearse at the funeral for Reverend Donald McDougall, long-time minister of Greenwood Church. At far right is Dr. John L. Bethune and facing the camera between the horse and wagon is Sam Cunard Campbell, governor of St. Paul Island. For almost thirty years MacAskill, a Baddeck entrepreneur and one of the town's first undertakers, helped residents through the difficult time of losing a loved one. (The MacAskill name remains connected with funeral services in Baddeck to this day with MacAskill's Funeral Home, operated by Charles's great-grandson, David Dunlop.)

Charles MacAskill was born in Big Baddeck in 1860, the son of Bennington and Elizabeth (McPhee) MacAskill. Sometime around 1900, he and his wife, Jessie (MacKay), moved their family to a home on the water side of Chebucto Street. The hayfield across the street, where he kept his horses and the funeral hearse, eventually became the driveway to the Alexander Graham Bell National Historic Site. MacAskill was father to Annabel, Bennington, and Bessie.

Charles's death certificate, signed by his daughter Annabel just days after he died in February 1950, at age ninety, noted that he continued working until he was eighty-eight years old.

One of Baddeck's early movers and shakers was H. Percy Blanchard (1862–1932), a civic-minded lawyer with progressive ideas that meshed well with those of Alexander Graham and Mabel Bell. It was likely Blanchard who spearheaded an effort to have the village government amend its bylaws to give Mabel Bell a vote on any civic matter in 1908—a full decade before women in Nova Scotia could mark a ballot and twelve years before any American woman could.

In a letter to Gilbert Grosvenor after Mabel Bell's death in 1923, Mr. Blanchard wrote: "When the Charter for incorporation of Baddeck Village was being prepared, we placed in it a clause giving an alien having property with the village, a vote the same as a citizen. Mrs. Bell, we knew, owned Gertrude Hall and it was to give her a vote, make her a citizen, that we framed the Charter."

During Blanchard's twenty-five years in Baddeck, he took an active role in the community as a trustee of Baddeck Public Library, as a member of the Baddeck Board of Commissioners, and as a bandleader for a brass band affiliated with the 94th Highlanders militia.

H. Percy Blanchard (middle), Janet Kidston (left), and Sam Campbell (right), February 23, 1909

As a lawyer during the heady days of aviation testing in Baddeck, Blanchard was, at times, the legal eyes and ears for the Aerial Experiment Association and the Canadian Aerodrome Company. Dealing with the legalese of the new technology likely appealed to the inventive side of the solicitor. He was a frequent visitor to Beinn Bhreagh, where he and Bell talked about developments in tetrahedral shapes, sheep breeding, and aircraft engines.

Blanchard's wife, Julia Calkin Blanchard (1863–1932), was also interested in the progressive movements in the community. She was a founding member of the Young Ladies Club of Baddeck and on the board of trustees of the Baddeck Public Library. The couple had five children.

In 1912, the Blanchards returned to Percy's father's home in Ellershouse, Nova Scotia, close to where both Percy and Julia were born and raised. There, he became an author, publishing books (including one about the McCurdys of Nova Scotia) and writing a regular column in the *Windsor Patriot* newspaper. He died in 1939.

Eccentric New Englander Benjamin Hoppin (1851–1923) moved to Baddeck in 1893, likely on the recommendation of Alexander Graham Bell. The writer and explorer settled in at Loughrea House on Water Street, one of the oldest homes in the village.

Benjamin was the son of James Mason Hoppin (1820–1906), a professor at Yale University and author of numerous books. When James died in 1906, he left Yale a substantial endowment of sixty thousand dollars to establish a chair in architecture, on the condition that Benjamin would be the first to fill it.

Benjamin accompanied Admiral Robert Peary on his 1896 expedition to the Arctic, as did A. H. Sutherland (owner of the Baddeck Steamship Company) and George Hollifield. On the trip roster, each man listed Baddeck as his hometown. (Also on the trek was African-American explorer Matthew Henson, who with Peary would successfully find the pole thirteen years later in 1909.) When the group returned south, Hoppin published the diary he kept during the trek.

A *New York Times* obituary in June 1923 describes Hoppin as an explorer who gained fame as a university student when he "accompanied Professor Marsh of Yale into the West in search of fossils." The expedition discovered a previously unknown, extinct genus of flightless aquatic birds in Kansas.

GEORGE AND JESSIE HOLLIFIELD, C.1915

When Benjamin Hoppin died, he left Loughrea House to his butler, George Hollifield (1878–1927), and the property became known as Hollifield House. George was extremely active in Baddeck life. He was the leader of the 94th Highlanders Regiment Band and an accomplished photographer. Born in Wales, Hollifield married Jessie Anderson (1875–1956) of Big Baddeck in June 1904. The couple lived in the waterfront home until their deaths.

**WILLIAM ROSS
MCASKILL, c.1915**

A long forgotten photo discovered between the pages of a dusty old book offers a brief glimpse into one man's all too short life.

The photo—in sepia shades—shows a handsome young man, leaning casually against the door jamb of a weather-beaten barn. It is summer, perhaps around haying time. He appears relaxed, as though just taking a break from work. His sleeves are rolled up, his hands rest casually in his pockets. His feet, clad in shiny black boots, are crossed coolly at the ankles. He is looking into the camera with a slightly inquisitive expression for the unknown photographer. A notation, written in the neat script of Mary (Jones) Bethune, simply states: "at the shack." On the back, another note written in Mary's son Tabby's (Dr. Clarence) loose scrawl: "W. R. McAskill at Farquhar McRae's Big Baddeck. Killed in first World War."

William Ross (W. R.) McAskill was the son of Ewen G. and Ermina (Minnie McKay) McAskill. Ewen operated the McKay, McAskill Store with his brother-in-law, Kenneth J. McKay. William was born December 5, 1890, and grew up in a building now called the Florence Apartments (behind the present-day Credit Union). He married Eira G. from Hazel Hill, Guysborough County, and became a businessman like his father and uncle, listing his profession as merchant on the attestation papers he signed in July 1916. William's sister, Marguerite, married Robert Jones Bethune, oldest son of Mary and Dr. John L. Bethune, that same year.

William McAskill served as a pilot with the Royal Flying Corps, no doubt influenced by fellow Baddeck resident J. A. D. McCurdy. Lieutenant McAskill was captured while serving overseas and died on June 19, 1917, less than a year after signing up. He was buried in the Hazebrouck Communal Cemetery in northern France.

On a warm June day at Beinn Bhreagh in 1917, Mabel Bell wrote to her mother and described a community's heartbreak at losing one of its sons:

"Our first Baddeck boy has gone, laid down his sunny red head that his little niece may inherit a free country….I sent his mother my best apple blossoms, rose-like flowers full two inches across. His mother said 'last year when Marguerite was married we had the apple blossoms…he was here and we were so happy.'"

MARGUERITE
(MCASKILL) BETHUNE
WITH DAUGHTER, RUTH,
1917

GEORGIE HALIBURTON MacLEOD, c.1925

Georgina Haliburton, the daughter of Thomas Andrew and Catherine (MacLeod) Haliburton, was born in 1870. She was a distant relative of novelist Thomas Chandler Haliburton. Her uncle was A. F. Haliburton, a lawyer who described the boundaries for Victoria County in 1851.

Georgie married Malcolm John MacLeod in 1897. For many years she was a member of the staff at Beinn Bhreagh and became a close associate of Mabel Bell.

In the 1901 census she was listed as a dressmaker. She became a member of the Bell Club in 1922.

George Kennan (1845–1924) brought the world to Baddeck through his stories of his travels around the world, tales of disasters, and accounts of assassinations. In 1891 he and Baddeck businessman Albert Hart decided Baddeck should have a library. He volunteered to present a lecture, with all proceeds going toward the purchase of books. There was yet no library to house them and nary a committee to run it. But few things intimidated George Kennan.

Kennan had trekked five thousand miles to Tsarist Russia three times in three decades, living for years in deepest Siberia where he observed Russian prisons and the exile system. He interviewed the survivors of a massive volcanic eruption on Mont Pelé, Martinique, where an estimated thirty thousand people died, providing eyewitness accounts for *Century Magazine.* He was the official White House correspondent in 1881, sending dispatches as President Garfield lay dying after being shot by an assassin. He was also a founding member of the National Geographic Society and a personal friend of Teddy Roosevelt, and it was Kennan's friendship with the Bells that brought Kennan and his wife, Emeline, to Baddeck.

In the late nineteenth century the first free public libraries began to open their doors to the populace in large cities. Philadelphia opened its own library in 1891, and New York in 1895. At the time, Nova Scotia had only one public library, in Halifax.

George Kennan's lecture at the Baddeck Courthouse on September 22, 1891, raised forty-seven dollars. Following his presentation, a committee was formed. It instructed Kennan to purchase books when he returned to Washington, D.C., that fall. Six weeks later, 141 volumes of "standard literature" arrived in Baddeck. That same day, the library committee met and drafted a constitution. Three months later, as the winter winds blew, Sheriff James Dunlop pushed his desk to one side to allow more room for a temporary library. For the next four years, the library patrons and those who needed the sheriff's services shared the space. In 1896, Mabel Bell donated space in Gertrude Hall for the library and reading room. Over the next thirty years, the Kennans often returned to Broadwater, their home on Baddeck Bay. George continued to travel the world, writing books about his excursions, and providing detailed reports to national magazines. Whenever he found himself in Baddeck, he offered free lectures to raise funds for the library.

Both Norman Bethune (1899–1986) and Gordon Stanley (G. S.) Harvey were entrepreneurs and involved in the development of the village. Harvey worked in the logging industry near St. Ann's and was renowned for his incredible strength. In 1949, Harvey became the first chairman of the volunteer committee that managed the new hospital. In 1954, as chair of the building committee, Harvey suggested that hospital auxiliaries be formed to help raise needed funds in Baddeck and the outlying districts. In the first few years of the hospital's operation, both Bethune's and Harvey's names frequently appeared on various volunteer committees.

At Bethune's Garage, a diesel engine and ten-kilowatt generator provided electricity to the village starting in 1926. By Christmas Eve of that year, four homes were wired for electricity. Nine months later, the plant's capacity had doubled, and Bethune added another engine and generator. By 1928, a third engine and generator were added, and the plant employed several people. Power lines ran along Chebucto to Water Street and for a half-mile down the Bay and Shore roads. Later, the lines ran to Twining and Queen streets.

The town's lights were turned on at dusk each evening and shut down at midnight. At 11:45 p.m., the lights were dimmed as a warning that the blackout was about to begin. Since Monday was a typical wash day, electricity was provided every Monday morning for five hours beginning at 7:00 a.m. Most homes paid an estimated $3.35 a month for electricity, while stores paid $8.00, and hotels $20.00.

In December 1939, a fire started in the power plant that could not be controlled. It destroyed Bethune's Garage, the electrical plant, and the Baddeck Public Library, which was located beside it.

**MARY MACDONALD,
1939**

Mary MacDonald (1848–?) took her memories of Baddeck across the continent, but spending more than half a century in California did not erase her Gaelic lilt. Mary was ninety-one years old when she was interviewed in 1939 by Sidney Robertson Cowell, a folk-music collector and researcher from Berkeley, California. In three brief snippets of interviews found at the Library of Congress in Washington, D.C., Mary MacDonald sings "Na cuperean," a Gaelic song about a barrel maker.

"He went over to sell the barrels to Baddeck," she said. "He has his sister—an old maid. Her name was Mary. When he'd go over to sell the barrels, he buy molasses and sugar and calico dresses for Mary, to dress her up before she is an old maid. Then the merchant in Baddeck, his name is Callum Campbell—he'd have a bill for this."

When Cowell asked if the occurrences in the songs really happened, Mary MacDonald replied: "Oh yes! I knew them and I went in their store. I knew the cooper!" She estimated the year to be 1871.

Only the barest biographical information is revealed during the interviews. Mary MacDonald was born in Cape Breton on November 15, 1848, married in 1872, and travelled in a covered wagon to California three years later.

"We came to stay in San Francisco. My husband had the asthma and we couldn't stay there. Then I had another baby before we left. Then I went to Nevada. I had six there," she said in the interview.

Dr. Clarence Bethune, c.1942

At the Queen Elizabeth II Health Sciences Centre in Halifax, the largest hospital complex in the Maritimes, stands a building named for the son of a country doctor. Dr. Clarence Bethune was on hand in 1968 to unveil the new name at a grand ceremony on the grounds of the teaching hospital. But the anaesthesiologist's proudest moment came in 1978 when Baddeck Academy students honoured him with a dinner and the title "Man for All Seasons."

He was christened Clarence in 1904, but anyone that knew him called him Tabby. The seventh son of Mary (Jones) and Dr. John L. Bethune, Clarence graduated from Dalhousie Medical School in 1931, fifty-six years after his father. He enlisted in the Medical Corp at the outbreak of World War II and helped to establish the Canadian General Hospital on the estate of Lord and Lady Astor.

In 1943, Bethune was named a member of the British Empire for his efforts. His friendship with the Astors continued after the war; in one letter, Lady Astor thanked Tabby and his mother for the care package they sent, in particular the butter, which was still rationed in the United Kingdom.

He was the administrator of the Victoria General Hospital in Halifax from 1945–1969, a period of great growth for the facility, as two new buildings were added to the complex. While in Halifax, he was involved in the Theatre Arts Guild and the very beginnings of the Neptune Theatre.

Clarence retired to his hometown of Baddeck in 1970 and threw himself into community matters—as president of the board of trade, as organist in two churches, as chairman of the Victoria County Museum and Archives, as vice-president of the Baddeck Public Library, and as a member of the Baddeck Rink Committee, where he spearheaded efforts to have an arena built. In 1976, "Tabby" was awarded the Order of Canada in recognition of his "exceptional contributions and service to the people of Nova Scotia." In 1984, he helped organize the visit of Prince Michael of Kent to mark the seventy-fifth anniversary of the flight of the Silver Dart, an event he witnessed in 1909.

Tabby loved history. He understood the importance of collecting and keeping records, letters, and photos so that future generations would have a tangible connection with their past. He had a way with words, and was unafraid to speak them.

During the first twenty years of Dr. C. L. "Monty" MacMillan's country practice in Victoria County, there was no hospital in the area, so the doctor tended to the sick in their homes, which could be anywhere from Iona to the foot of Smokey Mountain, a distance of some 140 kilometers. The trip, by horse and buggy, foot, snowshoe, and later in a motorized buggy similar to a snowmobile, was often arduous and could sometimes take days. To assist the doctor, residents began to hang lanterns on their gates to light the way and identify those who needed help.

After World War II, Dr. MacMillan (1903–1978) was instrumental in establishing the Victoria County Memorial Hospital in Baddeck. Named to honour soldiers from the county who fought in the war, the hospital was officially opened in 1949—the same year the doctor was elected to serve the residents of the county in the legislative assembly. Throughout Victoria County there were many "Montys" named in his honour, including a car ferry that once plied the Bras d'Or at Grand Narrows. In 1972, Dr. MacMillan was made a member of the Order of Canada.

In the late 1980s, as the community began fundraising to replace the aging hospital, the symbol adopted to represent the campaign was a lantern hung on a gate, an homage to Dr. MacMillan.

Other doctors that practiced in Baddeck in the nineteenth and early twentieth centuries included: Dr. Joseph Elmsley (1851–1859), Dr. S. G. A. McKeen (1860–?), Dr. John L. Bethune (1875–1913), Dr. Dan MacDonald (1894–1914), and Dr. John MacIvor.

Chapter 4

The Bell Family

THE BELL FAMILY IN WASHINGTON, D.C., 1885

It had been frantic. In the previous nine years, six months, and seven days, Alexander Graham Bell had invented a device that changed the world, married the love of his life, obtained unimaginable wealth, become a father, fought dozens of rivals wanting a piece of his invention and fortune, invented some more, and watched his wife don the black dress and veil of mourning for their two newborn sons, her two sisters, and her brother-in-law.

Now Bell wanted to take Mabel and their two daughters to a place far away, a peaceful, restful oasis. They searched in Massachusetts, Rhode Island, and New Jersey, but the peaceful place where they could build "a little cabin beside some running brook" eluded them.

By the summer of 1885, they still hadn't found it. Bell's father-in-law, Gardiner Greene Hubbard, suggested the family travel north to Cape Breton Island, where he had an interest in a coal mine. Gertrude Hubbard told her daughter that the island was filled with the most beautiful fir and spruce trees she had ever seen. Bell sought a copy of Charles Dudley Warner's 1874 travelogue, *Baddeck and That Sort of Thing*, to read en route. Their original itinerary included only a brief stopover in Baddeck before heading east to St. John's, Newfoundland, for two weeks. But that hopeful trip ended on the rocks outside St. John's when their ship, the *Hanoverian,* ran aground.

So they returned to Baddeck. After several idyllic days of fishing at the wharf, exploring the countryside, and going for moonlit walks, Mabel wrote in her journal: "Baddeck is certainly possessed of a gentle restful beauty and I think we would be content to stay here many weeks, just enjoying the lights and shades on all the hills and isles and lakes."

Paradise found.

After their brief two-week visit to Baddeck in 1885, the Bells returned in the summer of 1886.

The four-room house they rented (for five dollars a month) on Baddeck Bay was very different from their mansion on Scott Circle, just blocks from the White House, in Washington, D. C., but that was exactly what they had hoped for—a place where they could "live a simple, free and unconventional life."

During that first full summer in Baddeck Mabel wrote regularly to her mother, who was living in Washington:

> July 12, 1886: 'Our house is a mile and a half from the village…the air continues exhilarating and Alec enjoys it immensely and is full of plans for half a hundred things to be done when we are settled.'

> Aug 14, 1886: 'We met all the people going and coming from church and it was so nice that we knew nearly all the people so that Alec had to keep his hand near his hat. In the city you know the few acquaintances one has are so scattered and lost in the crowd so one feels a stranger in a strange place.'

Mabel, who had grown up in a wealthy, upper-class Cambridge, Massachusetts, family, threw herself into the varied chores associated with running a rural household. In early August 1886, she wrote: "Our jersey cow, Miss Miggs, is very pretty and I think will give us plenty of milk…My next investment is going to be a churn." A week later, she reported that the family used the churn for the first time:

> We all worked—Alec, the children and I…and after a long hard bout we had the delight of seeing our butter form. It did look like tightly scrambled eggs at first, but Nellie [the family's maid], who seems to know everything, soon brought it into shape and such beautiful yellow butter it became.…But we found the churning process less delightful in practice than in theory and Alec is trying to invent a windmill to do our churning for us.

Before the summer ended, the Bells purchased seventy acres of rolling hill at the point of Red Head. Not long after, it would be the location of their mansion, Beinn Bhreagh.

BADDECK BAY FROM RED HEAD, c.1890

In this photo, a horse-drawn wagon travels along a road at Red Head. Alexander and Mabel Bell often explored the Bras d'Or Lakes, rowing and sailing to the headland across the water from their Crescent Grove home. Arriving on the shore of Red Head—named for the reddish hue the setting sun cast on the peninsula—the Bells would hike past several farms to the top of the hill. The trek was exhausting, but once at the crest of the hill, the view and the fresh sea breeze lightened their steps.

"Fancy driving over the crest of a mountain—the highest for many miles and seeing the land stretched out on every side of you like a map. Hills and valleys, water and islands all around," Mabel Bell wrote of the experience.

From the mountaintop, they could see the enchanting view of St. Patrick's Channel with the gently sloping Washabuct Hill directly in front, the Great Bras d'Or and the edge of Boularderie Island to the east, the bluish Shenacadie Hills behind, and the Barra Strait in the distance.

During one hike to the top of the mountain, shortly after they purchased a thirty-acre section, they encountered the funeral of farmer Donald McAulay. Over the next few years, the Bells purchased Donald McAulay's land, and an additional four hundred acres on the point. The incident of McAulay's funeral stayed with Mabel. Some thirty years later, she wrote of the "dramatic incident as they, the incoming new masters descended the hill, the past old master was being borne forth from his house for the last time and they saw him laid to rest in the little graveyard on the hillside."

**BEINN BHREAGH,
c.1925**

RIGHT

**GARDENS AT BEINN
BHREAGH, WITH
GARDENER'S COTTAGE
BEHIND, c.1910**

In the summer of 1889, the Bells constructed a summer home across
Baddeck Bay from Crescent Grove. The Lodge was a chalet-style home,
built for warm summer days and nights and not equipped for winter's
chill. The family soon discovered that some of the unseasoned wood
used to build the house shrank, creating wide spaces between the boards
in some rooms. But the intrepid Bells decided to stay for Christmas in
1890, leaving only after much snow had fallen. Bundled into a large
sleigh, Mabel wrote of travelling by sleigh over the frozen lake: "We
drove around the head of the Bay and then across the ice from Baddeck
to Washabuct—our way being marked by little spruce trees set up in the
snow, and as the days were so very short, it took us three days to get to

the Strait of Canso and from there we took the train."

While summering at the Lodge, the Bells made plans for a larger home that would be used year-round. The spot for this grand house was the point at Red Head, a southwest-facing peninsula that juts into the Bras d'Or Lake. As Mabel expressed to her husband in April 1891, the gardens were a high priority: "I am most anxious to get the gardens there started as soon as possible. It will only take eighteen months or at the most two years to build the house, but five years is all too short an allowance for [a] garden to grow to real beauty."

The gardens flourished under her care; magnolia trees blossomed, and beech and pine trees grew to twice their normal size. During World War I, Mabel experimented with drying vegetables she had grown on the estate.

The house was a far cry from the little cottage they had originally envisioned on their first visit to Baddeck almost a decade earlier. The house at the point, now named Beinn Bhreagh Hall, was a grand, open-concept home, built for casual living. With thirty-seven rooms, there was ample space for the Bells, their extended family, and friends, and eventually, their ten grandchildren.

A SEA OF UMBRELLAS
OUTSIDE THE
COURTHOUSE,
OCTOBER 1897

In October 1897, the village was decorated for the visit of Lord Aberdeen, the governor general of Canada, and his wife, Lady Aberdeen, who was invited to speak to the Young Ladies Club of Baddeck about the Victorian Order of Nurses (VON), the group she had just established to provide nurses to rural areas.

Although the first branches were organized in large urban centres, such as Ottawa, Montreal, and Vancouver, Mabel and Alexander Bell immediately grasped the significance of the VON, and how it could benefit Baddeck. Victoria County was large and had only two doctors. A few nurses would help ease the burden of work on doctors Bethune and MacDonald.

After Lady Aberdeen spoke to the Young Ladies Club about the VON, both the Bells and the club championed the cause, and began working to get a nurse settled in Baddeck.

In June 1898, Alexander Graham Bell wrote that General Montgomery Moore, the commander in chief of the British Forces in Canada, was to address a public meeting about hiring a nurse for the community, "to urge the people to try the experiment for one year of supporting a trained nurse from Halifax." The community needed to raise four hundred dollars and form a committee. Bell, on behalf of an absent Mabel, offered to provide half the necessary funds to start. "I have no doubt that an important movement will be inaugurated, of great benefit to the country people here. The idea is good," he wrote. A committee was struck and Bell immediately stepped up, delivering a lecture, complete with lantern slides, on aerial navigation, with proceeds donated to the cause.

By 1899, when a diphtheria outbreak swept across the town, a nurse was in place.

VIEW FROM INDIAN POINT, C.1898

This portrait of Baddeck on the cusp of the twentieth century shows a rural community, with cows grazing in the fields around Baddeck Academy, on the left.

Alexander Graham Bell's very presence made Baddeck a hot spot for technological advancements and brought international attention to the village. Newspapers in New York, Washington, and beyond regularly featured stories about the Bells' far-reaching ideas and inventions, with Baddeck, Nova Scotia, in the dateline.

By 1898, the doors of Greenwood Church (visible as the larger church just to the left of centre) had been open for more than a decade. Another steeple visible on the main street is the Congregationalist Church; when it closed, Mrs. Bell bought the building and named it Gertrude Hall in honour of her mother. By 1898, it housed the Baddeck Public Library and hosted a number of public meetings and instructional classes over the years, including a short-lived fencing class taught by Kathleen, wife of Casey Baldwin.

HELEN KELLER FLYING A KITE AT BEINN BHREAGH WITH ALEXANDER GRAHAM BELL, 1901

Alexander Graham Bell met Helen Keller when she was only six years old. On his recommendation, she was enrolled at the Perkins Institute for the Blind in Boston. There she met Annie Sullivan, the teacher who finally connected with the blind and deaf child.

In August 1901, Helen, then twenty-one, was introduced to the women of the Young Ladies Club of Baddeck during a special meeting at Beinn Bhreagh Hall. She spoke to the group:

> People often ask me if I am happy. It seems strange to them that one who cannot see or hear should be able to enter into the joys of life. That is because they do not understand the power of love. By its magic one perceives that everything has its wonders—even darkness and silence. The eye cannot follow the flight of song; the ear cannot hear the music in the heart that receives it; but the spirit knows no limitation.

The next day she accompanied Bell to the kite field and held the string of a soaring box kite.

BELL WITH WORKERS AND LARGE TETRAHEDRAL KITE, 1902

From his earliest days as a boy in Scotland, Alexander Graham Bell was always interested in the notion of manned flight. As early as 1878, while on his honeymoon, he noted the different positions of seagulls' wings in flight. In the 1890s, he experimented with rocket power. The wide open fields at Beinn Bhreagh inspired him and soon his ideas took flight.

In 1903, Bell patented the tetrahedral cell, a strong and lightweight three-dimensional structure comprised of four triangular shapes. In these early aviation tests, his goal was to build a kite large enough to carry a man and a motor into the air, and stable enough to keep them there. Curious residents watched as the huge kites, some as big as a typical Baddeck home, soared above Beinn Bhreagh Mountain.

At the Beinn Bhreagh laboratory, carpenters built the ten-inch cells by the thousands, and seamstresses sewed the silk material to cover them. The cells were then built into large triangular and ring-shaped kites, and sometimes into other unusual groupings, to test drag and fly-ability.

By December 1906, worker Neil McDermid was lifted thirty feet into the air in a ten mile per hour breeze by the Frost King, a kite constructed with 1,300 tetrahedral cells.

MABEL HUBBARD BELL, TESTING THE PULL ON A KITE STRING, C.1905

Mabel Hubbard Bell (1857–1923) was a woman ahead of her time, and Baddeck benefited from her progressive ideas. She was born into wealth and privilege. Her father, Gardiner Greene Hubbard, was a patent lawyer and an entrepreneur who launched the first tramline from Cambridge to Boston. The Hubbards traced their ancestors to English royalty and to those who arrived on the *Mayflower*. Mabel's paternal grandfather, Samuel, was considered the richest man in Boston.

Mabel was an incredibly bright child. When she was almost five years old, she became deaf following a bout of scarlet fever. By the age of eight, she had become an expert lip-reader and was able to answer a series of questions about education of the deaf before the Massachusetts State Assembly. Her ability, at such a young age, helped pass two bills that led to the creation of a school for the deaf where students were taught to lip-read.

She and Bell seemed to find in each other the perfect match. She encouraged him, gently pushing him when he needed direction and offering suggestions about his many experiments.

In 1902, she posted a poem in the Beinn Bhreagh laboratory that quickly became the lab's motto:

If things seem a little blue,
Keep on fighting.
Stay it out and see it through,
Keep on fighting.

Do not give up in despair,
There will come a change somewhere.
Skies tomorrow will be fair
Keep on fighting.

Is the struggle hard and long?
Keep on fighting.
Face the music and be strong.
Keep on fighting.

Show your game and be proud of it
That you're not the sort to quit,
That you have old-fashioned grit.
Keep on Fighting.

To prove how strong and lightweight his tetrahedral design could be, Bell commissioned Frederick "Casey" Baldwin to build a lookout tower at the peak of Beinn Bhreagh Mountain.

Baldwin, a newly graduated mechanical engineer from Upper Canada, was a newcomer to Baddeck and a friend of J. A. D. McCurdy. The two young men had met at the University of Toronto, where they studied engineering. As McCurdy was readying to return to Baddeck for the summer of 1906, he asked Baldwin if he would like to spend a couple of weeks there, at the home of the inventor of the telephone. Within weeks of his arrival, Casey Baldwin and Alexander Graham Bell had designed the seventy-foot tripod tower and worked out the construction details.

Two legs of the tower, which formed a V-shape, were built on the ground. The third leg was assembled at the narrow end of the V, thus jacking the entire structure into the air. This ingenious method meant that no work was done at dangerous heights. The tower was built using

260 four-foot tetrahedral cells, each made from half-inch iron pipe. A stairway built into one of the legs allowed access to the lookout platform at the top.

On August 31, 1907, the tower opened with great fanfare. A newspaper clipping from the *New York Times* described the ceremony atop Beinn Bhreagh Mountain:

> They came in country wagons and carriages, driving, some of them, scores of miles across the hills to see the tetrahedral tower whose growth they had watched day by day from a distance. Hitching their teams to the fence posts they gathered beneath the fluttering flags of Canada (Royal Ensign) and the United States which decorated the tripod structure, and listened, bareheaded, to Mr. Bell as he stood with his tall form outlined against the background of sea and land, and told them how the idea of the tower originated as an outgrowth of his search for the lightest, strongest possible construction for his kites. Mr. Baldwin gave a brief description of the unique character of the tower and then formally turned it over to Mr. Bell by giving him the key to the stairway which leads to the platform at its apex.
>
> A bronze tablet...was then unveiled by Melville Bell Grosvenor, Mr. Bell's oldest little grandchild, who also unlocked the staircase door and invited the guests to 'Please come up.'

THE VIEW FROM THE
TOP OF THE TOWER,
c.1907

Alexander Graham Bell with Beinn Bhreagh lab workers, 1907

The Bell family hosted annual celebrations for Beinn Bhreagh workers and their families. The following is from a poster for the 1901 Harvest Home celebration:

> Held at Beinn Bhreagh
> On the Tennis Court (Above the Lodge)
> August 27, 1901, at 2 P.M.
>
> PRIZES IN ALL EVENTS.
>
> 1. Running and standing jumps for distance.
> 2. Running high jump
> 3. 50 yard dash for men
> 4. Putting the shot
> 5. Potato race
> 6. Obstacle race; this will include sack race, crawling through a barrel, climbing a fence, &c.
> 7. Harnessing and unharnessing single team
> 8. 50 yard run for ladies
> 9. Relay race between mixed couples; ladies run first; men do not start until partners have come in
> 10. Shooting contest
> 11. Tub race; wash-tubs used for boats, hands as oars
> 12. Boat race (from Warehouse to the Lodge)
> 13. Swimming race; 50 yards.
>
> DANCING IN THE EVENING AT THE WAREHOUSE.

In December 1907, the people of Baddeck witnessed the largest of Bell's kites, the Cygnet, taking flight over the Bras d'Or. Towed behind the steamer *Blue Hill*, it carried Thomas Selfridge, a member of Alexander Graham Bell's Aerial Experiment Association. Selfridge volunteered to ride the forty-two-foot-wide, motorless kite, constructed from over 3,300 tetrahedral cells.

The bootless Selfridge lay prone in the centre of the kite, dressed in light oilskins and covered with rugs. The tail end of a late-season hurricane was still whipping up whitecaps on the lake as the *Blue Hill* led the procession of small boats to the point off Beinn Bhreagh. From the rocking decks of the steamer, Mabel Bell and her two-year-old granddaughter, Mabel Grosvenor, watched as the *Blue Hill* towed a scow with the Cygnet on board.

J. A. D. McCurdy later described the joy on board the ship when the kite took flight:

> Well sir, the excitement from the top deck of the Blue Hill was something fierce. There was old Sam Campbell waving his bonnet and cheering like a madman. The Captain in his excitement blew the whistle half a dozen times and I feel sure that if there had not been so much noise we would have heard the snap of about a dozen cameras.... The fireman down in the boiler room realizing that we must get as much speed as possible, shoveled on a whole batch of coal causing dense black smoke to pour profusely from her funnels.

After an incredible seven-minute flight, the kite began to descend. At that moment, a blast of thick smoke from the *Blue Hill*'s smokestack obscured the view of the person charged with cutting the tow line. The backup plan of having Selfridge cut the line also failed because his view was obstructed by the kite. The *Blue Hill* continued towing the Cygnet at full speed; the kite was demolished and Selfridge was tossed into the freezing Bras d'Or.

After several tense moments, Selfridge was found "swimming for his life, impeded of course by the clothing he wore," according to Alexander Graham Bell. "[Selfridge] immediately relieved our anxiety, by calling out 'It's all right, It's all right.'" He was taken aboard a rescue boat and whisked to the *Blue Hill* where a heated cabin and a doctor were waiting for him.

Sadly, just months later in September 1908, Selfridge became the world's first aviation fatality. During a test flight with Orville Wright in Virginia, a propeller snapped and the plane crashed. Orville Wright was badly injured, and Thomas Selfridge died later in hospital.

ALEXANDER GRAHAM
BELL LEAVING THE
BEINN BHREAGH
LABORATORY, C.1908

In settling into life in Cape Breton, Alexander Graham Bell instituted Wednesday night meetings at Beinn Bhreagh. He had hosted similar evenings at his home in Washington, D. C., that were attended by eminent scientists, explorers, and politicians. He described the Cape Breton version in a letter to his wife in June 1894:

> Club meeting tonight, 40 persons present, most quite young men. Good many came from town. I described Edison's kinetoscope, also spoke of eclipses of the sun and moon illustrating by means of our large globe for the earth, a big lamp for the sun, and a boy's ball for the moon. Mr. Kennan gave a Siberian experience which interested all greatly. Mr. Kennan, Mr. McCurdy and Josie (Joseph) McLean poured forth a perfect volume of anecdotes, jokes etc, which kept us all in a roar. Then we had music interspersed all through. Cornet and piano, Ellis and AGB. Bagpipes by a Mr. McDonnell of Middle River. Gaelic song, in volume by the crowd. Gaelic dancing to the bagpipes and fiddle. Two fiddlers present.

GILBERT GROSVENOR,
c.1930

Gilbert Grosvenor (1875–1966) was one of the early innovators of modern photojournalism. Born in Constantinople, Turkey (today called Istanbul), Grosvenor was the son of a university history professor. In 1899 Alexander Graham Bell, then president of the decade-old National Geographic Society, hired the bespectacled twenty-four-year-old Grosvenor as an editorial assistant for the society's magazine. (A year later in October 1900, Grosvenor sealed his connection to the famous family by marrying the Bells' oldest daughter, Elsie.)

Over his fifty years as editor and then president, Grosvenor took the society's membership from nine hundred to two million and published previously unknown glimpses of Russia, the Arctic, and the Far East. In the summer of 1909, as Grosvenor pieced together the latest edition of the magazine at his makeshift office at Beinn Bhreagh, a telegram arrived. Arctic explorer Robert Peary informed Grosvenor that his National Geographic–funded expedition to the Arctic had arrived at the North Pole.

Students visit Beinn Bhreagh labs, 1909

Students from Baddeck Academy were welcome visitors to the Beinn Bhreagh labs. Just days before the Silver Dart took flight in 1909, the students in this image received a tour of the aviation headquarters. While there, Bell asked them to name an experimental motorized tetrahedral kite. They christened it the Cygnet II.

Later that year, the Canadian Aerodrome Company welcomed a large number of curious Baddeck residents to view the airplane *Baddeck I,* as recorded in Bell's notes for July 9:

> Mr. Douglas McCurdy presided upon the occasion and exhibited the new aerodrome that has just been completed by the Company, the first built by them. He stated that this was the first aerodrome of exclusively Canadian manufacture and that it had been made entirely by Baddeck men. For this reason the company had given the people of Baddeck the opportunity of seeing it before its departure for Petawawa where it will be fitted with an engine. To mark the place of its origin the machine will officially be known as the aerodrome 'Baddeck No. 1.'

> After the exhibition the visitors adjourned to Mrs. Baldwin's bungalow where afternoon tea was presided over by Mrs. Frost, a sister of Mr. Douglas McCurdy and by Miss Georgina McCurdy [J. A. D.'s aunt].

In the days leading up to the historic flight, the Beinn Bhreagh lab was a beehive of activity. In the village, people spoke of the weather and flying machines. By February 23, all the pieces were falling into place. The plane was assembled. The engine was tested and installed. The AEA members were on hand and ready to watch history in the making.

On the morning of that cold winter day, residents assembled on the frozen bay to watch the trials. Bell, concerned about the safety of the growing crowd, posted notices at regular intervals on the ice that warned spectators to not "on any account place themselves in the path of the machine." Regardless, there are several accounts of curious residents standing before the oncoming plane, then stepping out of its way with just moments to spare. After a single flight of three-quarters of a mile, at a height of sixty feet, McCurdy landed. For him, the jaunt was simply a test run. For Bell and everyone else watching, the flight made history, bringing Canada into the age of aviation.

In telegrams announcing the flight to the *Sydney Post*, the *Halifax Herald*, the *London Times*, and the Associated Press, Bell proudly announced "the town of Baddeck as witness" to the momentous flight, and he ensured that the names of the 147 Baddeck residents who observed the flight were recorded for posterity in the *Beinn Bhreagh Recorder*.

The next day, the village board of commissioners met to express congratulations to Bell, the AEA, and "bold aeronaut Douglas McCurdy, a Baddeck boy born and bred."

The flights continued for the next month and Baddeck continued to watch. As McCurdy tested the endurance of the Silver Dart, he winged past the homes and businesses in the village to an upright spruce tree planted in the frozen ice in St. Patrick's Channel, just west of the town, where he would make a wide turn and wing back towards Beinn Bhreagh. At Baddeck Academy, students heard the whine of an engine and raced to the windows to McCurdy and the Silver Dart zooming past.

A month after the historic flight, the Parents' Association of Baddeck hosted a lecture on aviation where McCurdy told the crowd at the packed courthouse: "As time goes on and Canada gains more and more prominence in the eyes of the aeronautical world, the citizens of Baddeck can look back and be proud that their home town was instrumental in introducing aviation into the Dominion."

**THE YOUNG LADIES
OF BADDECK CLUB,
DRESSED TO PERFORM A
PLAY, C.1910**

Left to right: Ella Watson, Hazel (Morrison) Manchester, Mrs. Malcolm
McLeod, Bessie (McAskill) Dunlop, Sadie (McLeod) Currie, Louise
MacDonald.

Mabel Bell was inspired.

Sitting in the morning room of a senator's home with a handful of
other Washington, D. C., women in 1891, Mabel Bell was inspired.
The very notion that women were meeting informally to discuss current events and learn about the world around them was a foreign one,
and participating in such a meeting was empowering.

It was the beginning of a progressive era in women's rights, one
that culminated almost thirty years later with the right to vote. But
until then, most women were marginalized. A polite woman would
never voice an opinion, especially a controversial one, in public. In
fact, decorum of the straitlaced Victorian era prescribed that a well-
mannered woman would not even speak in public.

So the very notion of forming a club where women could learn
about the outside world was audacious and more than a little bold.
"When our name was under discussion, I remember longing to call it
just the Baddeck Club and not daring, lest the men might object to the
women taking possession of the village name….We were not women
suffragists then," Mabel Bell recalled in 1911 during the club's twentieth anniversary celebrations.

On a cool autumn evening, Baddeck women and young ladies gathered at the Lodge to "stimulate the acquisition of general knowledge and to promote sociability." The women were expected to conduct research, write papers, and then present the information to the members. The idea was embraced by the women in Baddeck, who were soon learning about life in Siberia and the move to present a modern Olympics in Greece. But gathering information for presentations in rural Cape Breton was not an easy task: "The public library was not then started. We were such a little village, [far] from the nearest railway station…There were no big maps. We made them on wrapping paper and hung them on curtains to illustrate current events. None of us had ever spoken in public before and it required real pluck to begin," Mabel Bell wrote.

As the club celebrated its thirtieth anniversary in 1921, Mabel Bell concluded her presentation by stating: "Among my dearest memories are meeting with the people of Baddeck."

After Alexander Graham Bell died in August 1922, the club was renamed the Alexander Graham Bell Club. While some members sought to name the club in honour of its founder, Mabel Bell declined. The club has held meetings continuously since 1891, making it the longest-running women's club in Canada.

**INTERIOR SUN PORCH AT
BEINN BHREAGH HALL,
1915**

From the sun porch at Beinn Bhreagh, observers could watch sailboats passing on the lake below. Just outside, at the east end of the Beinn Bhreagh lawn, was an observatory, where in May 1898 Bell observed "a glorious view of Jupiter," reporting that he could "make out his cloud belts and four of his five moons." Another of Bell's telescopes is visible at the right of this photo.

INTERIOR GREAT ROOM AT BEINN BHREAGH HALL, 1915

Around this massive fireplace the ideas flew. Alexander Graham Bell held court here with his aviation associates—J. A. D. McCurdy, Casey Baldwin, Thomas Selfridge, and Glenn Curtiss—seated around him. Following one particular brainstorming session, Mabel Bell suggested that the group organize formally, and she later financed the group with thirty-five thousand dollars. Over the next eighteen months, the Aerial Experiment Association (AEA) built two large kites and four powered flying machines.

Each of its members made history: Tom Selfridge as the pilot of the kite Cygnet in December 1907; Casey Baldwin as the first Canadian to fly (in Hammondsport, New York) in March 1908; Glenn Curtiss as the pilot of the first public flight of a kilometre in America (which earned the AEA the first Scientific America Award); J. A. D. McCurdy as the pilot of the Silver Dart, the first heavier-than-air flying machine to take flight in Canada in 1909; and Mabel Bell as the first woman to finance research and development in the field of aviation.

In a 1908 article describing the work of the AEA, J. A. D. McCurdy wrote: "Every afternoon when work was over at the laboratory we gathered around the big fireplace at Dr. Bell's home where the events of the day were discussed over a cup of afternoon tea. Here the whole family gathered, Mrs. Bell, grandchildren and all and it was one of the most delightful moments of the day."

One of the last major experimental projects undertaken at the Beinn Bhreagh labs was the hydrofoil.

By the time the HD-4 was breaking world records on the Bras d'Or Lake, Alexander Graham Bell was seventy-one years old. He was not interested in speeding across the waves of the Bras d'Or Lake in a five-ton behemoth of a boat. Those were experiments for the young.

Mabel, however, was more adventurous. In November 1919, at age sixty-one, she took the wheel of the HD-4, steering it on Baddeck Bay, with Casey Baldwin as co-pilot.

Bell watched fretfully from the wharf. "It was a most wonderful trip," she later wrote. The HD4 "felt like a rock, so steady and kept on an even keel."

MABEL BELL'S
HYDROFOIL RIDE,
NOVEMBER 1919

The Bells' very presence brought high-level scientists, politicians, explorers, innovators, and business people to town, and the couple often organized public meetings so that residents could hear from these distinguished visitors. Topics included such wild and far-off things as George Kennan's travels to (and subsequent exile from) Siberia; Samuel Langley's aviation experiments with unmanned steam-powered aircraft; and explorer John Wesley Powell's tales as the first non-Native to explore the Grand Canyon.

Having access to such wide-ranging and innovative ideas opened the minds of those living in the small rural community. Both Alexander and Mabel Bell called Baddeck home, and a number of their innovations and ideas came to light here, forever cementing the community's place in history. Over the years, Alexander and Mabel were instrumental in developing a number of firsts at Baddeck. Highlights include:

> 1891—Canada's oldest continuing women's club forms at
> Beinn Bhreagh
> 1891—Second library in Nova Scotia formed
> 1897—Early use of Victorian Order of Nurses in Canada
> 1895—First home and school association in Canada
> formed at Baddeck Academy
> 1907—First flight of Cygnet, a man-carrying kite
> 1909—The Silver Dart flies, the first flight of heavier-than-
> air machine by a British subject
> 1909—The first aircraft manufacturing company in Canada
> formed at Baddeck

1917—First Montessori School in Canada established at
Beinn Bhreagh

1919—Fastest marine craft in world, the HD-4, built at
Baddeck

The ties between the Bell family and the community continued
after the deaths of Alexander Graham and Mabel Bell, when a museum
dedicated to the inventor opened at Baddeck in 1956.

A great chapter in the history of Baddeck came to an end at 2:00
A.M. on August 2, 1922, when Alexander Graham Bell died. His wife,
Mabel, daughter Daisy, and son-in-law David Fairchild had gathered
around him. His last view was of the moon rising above the mountain
he loved.

"No one could wish for a more beautiful ending," Daisy later wrote
to her sister Elsie, who was travelling in South America when the
end, caused by complications from diabetes, came unexpectedly. "He
was on the porch, with the fresh air about him and it was a beautiful
moonlit night….'How beautiful it is here, the air is so fresh,' he said in
the afternoon and he just breathed more deeply and more slowly until
finally he didn't breathe again."

Two days later, at five o'clock in the afternoon, Bell was buried on
top of Beinn Bhreagh Mountain. The service was simple and informal.
His gravesite, under the tetrahedral tower and overlooking the wide
expanse of the Bras d'Or, had been chosen by Bell himself many years
earlier, when he spent a few hours lying in various poses on the mountaintop.

His coffin was made of Beinn Bhreagh pine at the Beinn Bhreagh
laboratory by men who had worked side by side with the inventor
for years. It was lined with the same red silk that covered his tetrahedral kites. After a short service in Beinn Bhreagh Hall for the family,
Bell made his last trip to the mountaintop, his coffin on a buckboard
wagon as pallbearers walked slowly beside. Mabel Bell asked that
no one wear black, the traditional colour of mourning. Instead, she

wanted her husband's life to be celebrated. Reverend John MacKinnon of Greenwood Church delivered a short eulogy. Those gathered sang "Bringing in the Sheaves," and soloist Jean MacDonald, a favourite singer of Bell's, sang a verse from Robert Louis Stevenson's poem, "Requiem":

> Under a wide and starry sky,
> Dig the grave and let me lie.
> Glad did I live and gladly die
> And I lay me down with a will.

At the end of the funeral, all phone service across North America was suspended for one minute.

A year later, also at five o'clock in the afternoon, Mabel Bell's ashes were laid to rest beside her husband. She died on January 3, 1923, in Washington, D. C., just five months after her husband. Her official cause of death was pancreatic cancer, but most who knew her said Mabel died of a broken heart.

Chapter 5

The School and Churches

BADDECK ACADEMY, C.1890

THE SCHOOL

S partan, plain, austere—this early photo of Baddeck Academy shows
few outward signs of extravagance. But within these hallowed halls,
an enduring movement was created when parents and teachers
formed the first home and school association in Canada in 1895.

A school, of course, is so much more than just a place to learn reading, writing, and arithmetic. It becomes the heart of a community, where hopes and dreams for the future dwell.

Shortly after Baddeck was designated the shiretown of the new County of Victoria in 1851, a school was established. But it was not the town's first. Some thirty years earlier, Hezekiah Ingraham, a Big Baddeck cooper, set a room aside in his small log home and hired a teacher for his three children. Soon word of the school spread, and Ingraham opened the doors to any student interested in education.

Robert Elmsley makes just a few passing references to the earliest days of a school within the bounds of Baddeck village: "May 26, 1857. Fine day. School meeting. Trustees appointed." In June 1861, a new schoolmaster was appointed, but surprisingly, Elmsley did not record his name.

The Academy on Shore Road was built about 1880. A 1904 report by John MacKinnon, inspector of schools for Victoria County, noted that an extension at the school was under construction. "The structure will practically be a new building and will afford ample and commodious accommodation for years to come," he wrote.

In a 1972 letter, Baddeck resident Alex MacLean recalled Baddeck Academy's four classrooms each had a beehive stove for heat. Thirsty students had to get permission to go to a neighbouring home for a glass of water; years later a corner shelf was built in each classroom to accommodate a galvanized pail and dipper for drinking water. MacLean described many of the students, especially boys, wearing "moggins": "They were made by putting a wool slipper over several pairs of socks. They were very warm and were generally worn by pupils who would have to walk some distance to reach school."

Margaret Janet McPhee was inspired by the progressive ideas of Alexander and Mabel Bell, and as the first female principal at Baddeck Academy, she was a driving force in the organization of Canada's first home and school association.

She recognized and valued the educational resource of the inventor's laboratories at nearby Beinn Bhreagh and often took classes to visit. It was there, in 1897, that Bell demonstrated the new X-ray machine he had imported, capturing the skeletal image of McPhee's hand.

Born in Antigonish County to Ann (MacLean) and Archibald, a blacksmith, McPhee attended Dalhousie University, where she earned both bachelor and master of arts degrees. In July 1897, while dining at Beinn Bhreagh Hall, McPhee met Sarah Fuller, head schoolmistress for the Horace Mann School for the Deaf in Boston.

"Miss Fuller is very much pleased with Miss McPhee," Mabel Bell later wrote to her husband. "She said she was very courteous and careful in expressing herself, looking ahead to where her words would fall. She told her she would like her for a teacher of the deaf, but I said we could not spare her."

In 1898 McPhee married Dr. Edward Hart, son of Charles, a merchant, and Ellen (Baxter) of Baddeck. They settled in Victoria, British Columbia.

The individuals in the photo are identified as: *back row, left to right*: Miss McPhee, Annie Bentick, [first name unknown] Reid, Janie Taylor, Jessie Campbell, Garfield McKay, Watson girl from Bras d'Or, Emily Taylor, Harold Atwater, Malcolm McKenzie; *middle row*: Alex McAulay, John McKinnon, Phillip J. P. McLeod, Willie McDonald, Fred McInnis, Aubrey Atwater, Fraser boy, Harvey Rice; *front row*: Jean McDougall, Jean Campbell, Sybil Tremaine, Mae Campbell, Janie McDonald, Jessie McDonald.

TEACHERS AND PUPILS, c.1900

Identified in this photo are, back row: sixth from left, John R. McLeod; sixth from right, Agnes "Aggie O" McLean; middle row: second from left, Jean McDougall; second from right, Florrie J. P. (McLeod); far right, C. "Tena O" McLean; front row: second from left, Tosh McLeod; middle, Roddie Bethune; and far right, Ian MacDonald.

In an effort to establish schools in rural districts, in 1826 the province recommended that an annual schoolmaster's salary be about fifty pounds. Most districts were paying between thirty-five and forty pounds. Baddeck offered forty pounds a year, but half was payable in produce, according to *Beyond the Atlantic Roar: a Study of the NS Scot* by Donald Campbell and R. A. McLean.

In 1865, Victoria County had twenty-eight male and thirty-three female teachers. Of those, only four (two men and two women) had first-class teaching licenses.

Typical course offerings for students in 1901 included spelling and diction, reading and elocution, bookkeeping, geography, history, practical mathematics, moral and patriotic duties, and hygiene and temperance.

In the fall of 1909, this class had a field trip to Beinn Bhreagh. Mabel
Bell was an ardent supporter of early education for children and often
invited students and teachers to visit the gardens at the Bell's nearby
estate. After classes ended on September 27, three teachers and seventy-
three students boarded Bell's sailboat *Gauldrie* at Baddeck, and landed
near the foot of Beinn Bhreagh Mountain. Mrs. Bell, her daughter
Elsie Grosvenor, and Mabel's first cousin Caroline McCurdy met the
group on the grounds at Beinn Bhreagh, then proceeded to give the
group a tour of the estate's large flower gardens. Christine MacLennan
wrote of the trip in the *Beinn Bhreagh Recorder*:

> The younger children were allowed to play with Miss
> McCurdy's dog "General Wolf." From the garden the
> children were taken to see the Scotland pony and the Zulu
> sheep. The boys were very much taken with the Zulu sheep
> and admired them for their horns. On returning the Beinn
> Breagh Hall the children were shown into the dining room
> where refreshments were served...Mrs. Bell gave each one
> of the children a large bouquet of flowers cut from her
> garden. They all said they had a fine time and enjoyed the
> sail back to Baddeck in the moonlight.

The individuals in the photo are identified as: first row (left to
right): Douglas Fraser, Alexander McDonald, Clarence Bethune,

Sherman Bedwin, Fred Haliburton, Joe McNeil, Warren Gilman, Archie McDonald, Blair Crowdis, Murdock Kelly, Johnnie Gillis, Dan Campbell, Murdock Stewart.

Second row (left to right): Catherine MacAulay, Margaret McKay, Ollie McRae, Minnie McAskill, Greta Taylor, Lillian McLean, Ada Haliburton, Laura Kelly, Christy Stewart, Lexina Stewart, Margaret Kelly, Miss E. Watson, Isabelle Gilman with teacher Rhoda McLeod, Eleanor Blanchard, Alice McFarlane, Harold Haliburton (on steps), Mary McKenzie, McIvor (first name unknown), Cecilia McNeil, Edith McAulay, Flemming (first name unknown), Mary Morrison.

CHURCHES

Under the hot midsummer sky in July 1885, construction began on the new Greenwood Presbyterian Church. Unlike Knox Presbyterian, its predecessor built along Baddeck Bay nearly forty years earlier, this new place of worship was positioned just steps from the main intersection in town, where the roads from Red Head, Whycocomagh, St. Ann's, the Margarees, Middle River, and Big Baddeck met. This new church owed its name to a long-forgotten chapel built in a grove of evergreens at the northwest edge of the village (near the present-day hospital).

It was a busy time in Baddeck, with new construction and new ideas. A new rail bed with track was laid on Charles J. Campbell's wharf to assist the shipbuilding industry. At the eastern corner of Chebucto and Jones streets, men excavated—with picks and shovels—the foundation of a new customs house and post office, while stonemasons dressed the stones stacked nearby.

Even the oft-restrained publication the *Presbyterian Witness* got caught up in the boom-time atmosphere, stating that the handsome new church was "intended to accommodate between six and seven hundred people." Dan Stewart, a Greenwood historian, notes in his 1976 unpublished history that, including the balcony and some extra chairs, the church's capacity was closer to three hundred.

As the church neared completion, the builders added an octagonal spire that rose twenty-seven metres and was topped with a weather vane. Sailors rounding the point at Red Head used the steeples of Greenwood and St. Michael's to navigate the channel into Baddeck Harbour.

In 1925, following the nationwide merger of Presbyterian, Methodist, and Congregational churches, Greenwood Presbyterian became Greenwood United Church.

The following table displays how Baddeck residents identified their religious affiliations, as indicated on the 1881 census (and as compiled by Baddeck postmaster Robert Elmsley).

Religion in Baddeck, 1881

Baptist	39
Bible Christian	4
Catholic	133
Church of England	114
Church of Scotland	29
Congregationalist	38
Freewill	1
Methodist	55
Presbyterian	1343
Reformer	2
Unitarian	4
other denominations	3

Reverend Donald McDougall's sermons turned many skeptics into staunch believers. When McDougall was ministering in West and Cow bays, people came from far and wide to hear his uplifting revivals. His reputation followed him to Baddeck; in 1893, the Greenwood Church trustees noted that just one year after his arrival, the congregation had grown by more than thirty families.

Born in Whycocomagh in 1837, McDougall married Barbara Boak in 1868 in Halifax. His early pastoral charges were in Prince Edward Island and Port Morien, where his three daughters, Florence (1872–1948), Harriet (1874–1949), and Jean (1883–1955), were born.

In addition to conducting the customary Sunday services, christenings, marriages, and funerals, McDougall also held weekly prayer meetings for congregations in Big Baddeck, Rear Big Baddeck, Inlet Baddeck, Red Head, Plaister Mines, and Baddeck Bridge. Twice a month he also conducted morning and evening services in Gaelic.

In the spring of 1893 Alexander Graham Bell noted that the "Presbyterians are indulging in a Pink Tea—raising money to build a new manse for Reverend McDougall near the new church." A year later, the minister and his family were settled in the manse, built by contractors Rhodes and Curry, the same Amherst company responsible for constructing Beinn Bhreagh Hall in 1893.

Just before Reverend McDougall retired in 1907 after serving Baddeck for sixteen years, the congregation happily noted that it was out of debt and in the black, as the church and manse were both paid for in full. The 1907 annual report concluded that it was "the best year in the history of the congregation."

MOURNERS AT REVEREND DONALD MCDOUGALL'S FUNERAL, GREENWOOD CHURCH, MAY 1908

Mourners gather beside Greenwood Church for the funeral of the former minister Reverend Donald McDougall, May 8, 1908. (Tom Roberts, the boy, is the only person identified in the photo). The Masonic Hall spire can be seen in the background. News of McDougall's death appeared in the *Sydney Daily Post* on May 5, 1908:

> The death occurred yesterday at St. Joseph's Hospital Glace Bay, of the Reverend Donald McDougall, late pastor at Broughton....The late Mr. McDougall was the former pastor at Baddeck and had been (at Broughton) recently attending the induction of Rev. C. C. McIntosh. He was returning to Broughton, but was taken ill at Glace Bay and as removed to the hospital. Mrs. McDougall (Barbara Boak) and her daughter, Mrs. George F. (Florence) McRae of Baddeck were with Mr. McDougall during his illness and they will accompany the remains to Baddeck today. The interment will take place on Thursday. The late Mr. McDougall was pastor at Port Morien and West Bay.

THE FIRST KNOX PRESBYTERIAN CHURCH, BAY ROAD, C.1902

In 1841, with just a handful of residents settled on the five-kilometre stretch from Kidston Island to the head of Baddeck Bay, the Presbyterian congregation built a church.

At first, the church's nearest neighbour was Hector MacLean, whose log cabin was to the east. Eventually, Joseph Elmsley built Sackville House, a single-storey, double-chimney, whitewashed house to the west. For fifteen years, the congregation was without a full-time minister. The small flock of Scotch Presbyterians was tended to by Reverend Alexander Farquharson from Middle River and Reverend James Fraser from Boularderie.

In 1849, a group of residents (Mrs. Kidston, Miss J. MacLean, Ronald MacDonald, Farquhar MacRae, John Buchanan, Mrs. Taylor, Donald MacAulay, Mr. and Mrs. Charles J. Campbell, Miss K. Ingraham, Mrs. John Watson, and Alexander Taylor, church treasurer) made a donation of thirteen pounds, seventeen and one-half pence to the Free College in Halifax, presumably to persuade the powers that be to assign a minister. Six years later, Reverend Kenneth MacKenzie took charge of the pulpit in 1856.

Today all that remains of the first church built in Baddeck is the stone foundation, surrounded by the graves of some of the village's earliest settlers, including Dunlop, Elmsley, Campbell, Jones, and Kidston.

**KNOX CHURCH,
c.1900**

Mary Blatchford visited her cousin Mabel Bell at Beinn Bhreagh twice, first in 1891 and again a decade later in 1911, each time writing detailed letters to her friends and family back home in Massachusetts. During one visit she witnessed a week-long religious ceremony called the Sacrament at Knox Church, where the little church was filled past capacity with people standing in the outer porch and lined along the outside stairs. The churchyard and the "green beyond was nearly as full of wagons and horses tied to fences and trees," Blatchford wrote.

> After the Sacrament came the singing, which how will I describe—for it was like nothing I had ever heard before. They sang a Psalm with ever-so-many verses, the presenter leading off the first few words of each verse alone and the rest joining in all on the same note—there was no singing part. As for a tune—if tune it could be called, it was more like the music of a bagpipe with all the harshness taken out. The voices rose and fell in an almost unearthly sweetness and pathos, swelling and dying away again until the tears came to my eyes. No music ever affected me as that did....I heard some preaching and praying and was fascinated with the musical richness of the unpronounceable gutturals.... One word seemed to be forever to the fore 'haggis' and I felt so familiar with it that I was conscious of a certain uplifting of the soul whenever it came. Was it 'Lord'? Or 'heaven'? Or 'faith' or 'hope' or 'love'? I meant to ask....I wondered how long it would take to understand the whole sermon, for I felt that I knew the spirit of haggis already.

When Blatchford met a Gaelic teacher the following day, she asked him what "haggis" means: "He looked puzzled and shook his head and did not know what it might be. But I insisted that the minister used it all the time 'haggis this' and 'haggis the other' and 'haggis' again and again. And there came a twinkle in his grave eyes and with a gentle laugh he said 'Oh, you mean ahgeese. It means *and*.'"

Overlooking Chebucto from its perch on the north side of the street, the spire of St. Michael's can be seen rising above the trees in many old photos.

The first St. Michael's Church on this site was built in the mid-nineteenth century and dedicated in 1858. According to a 1943 church history by Alex McLean, the church bell used to call parishioners to worship weighed two hundred pounds and was salvaged from a ship-wreck near Inverness. When the bell was replaced in 1888, it was retired to a position in the rafters above the organ. The new bell, from the McShane Bell Foundry in Baltimore, Maryland, tolled in the early morning hours of September 6, 1926, to warn residents of the fire that engulfed much of the eastern end of town.

The parishioners saved most of the church's valuables from the fire, with the exception of the two bells. McLean wrote: "I often regret that I had not thought of this small bell in the morning of the fire, as it could have been removed very easily, but in the attendant excitement and in the rush and bustle of removing the sacred vessels, vestments and ornaments, it was never thought of."

The church was rebuilt on the same site and dedicated in August 1928 with a new bell from the Henry Stuckstede Bell Foundry in St. Louis, Missouri.

St. Peter-St. John Anglican Church, c.1920

Reverend Simon Gibbons was tenacious. Known as the first Inuit priest, he believed in taking the word of the Lord to the people—no matter that the people were in isolated communities hundreds of miles apart. In the summer, he walked over one hundred miles from Baddeck to Neils Harbour and back again to preach. In the winter, he'd snow-shoe, often arriving exhausted. But his charisma combined with his good looks helped him attract followers and funds.

Born in Labrador to an Inuit mother and a white father, Gibbons was orphaned by the age of six. He was raised in orphanages operated by the Church of England, and eventually adopted by a bishop of the church in Newfoundland.

Not only could Gibbons round up needed donations, but he could also swing a hammer and help with construction. As a result, he oversaw the construction of a number of churches over his life. The distinctive "Gibbons's tower" can be found on churches in both Nova Scotia and Prince Edward Island. One of the churches Gibbons helped construct was St. Peter–St. John in Baddeck. In August 1883, as the temperature nudged one hundred degrees, the little church was conse-crated with about 126 people in attendance. Robert Elmsley's daughter Florence and Judge Tremain's daughter Kate were both confirmed by the Anglican bishop during the event.

KNOX PRESBYTERIAN CHURCH,   BADDECK, N.S.

THE SECOND KNOX PRESBYTERIAN CHURCH, GRANT STREET, C.1925

A portion of the Presbyterian congregation decided to remain independent when three churches merged in 1925. This group built Knox Presbyterian Church on Grant Street in 1926. The new church was named to honour the first church built at Baddeck in 1841.

Chapter 6

Public Officials and Public Buildings

BADDECK JAIL, C.1880

Writer Charles Dudley Warner described the "gaol" as a whitewashed stone building, a storey and a quarter tall, on the main street of Baddeck. Warner wrote that it was "retired a little from the road, with a square of green turf in front of it," adding that he "should have taken it for the residence of the dairyman's daughter, but for the iron gratings at the lower windows. A more inviting place to spend the summer in, a vicious person could not have."

The jailer's family, a growing brood, had taken over the front jail cell, "a cheerful room commanding a view of the village street and of the bay," Warner wrote. One newspaper account reported that the jail was used for visitors when no rooms were available in any of the village hotels.

In March 1899, the *Baddeck Telephone* carried a rare report of crime in Baddeck: There had been a burglary at Beinn Bhreagh Hall. The culprit's footprints led from the point, across the frozen Bras d'Or, to Shenacadie, where the trail grew cold. There was a break, however, a few days later when the robber was found hiding in Margaree. A revolver, a rifle, and "some other odds and ends found on the prisoner were identified by witnesses as belonging to Mr. Bell or Mr. (Arthur) McCurdy and one witness was of the opinion that the trousers then on the prisoner had previously been worn by Charles Thompson, Mr. Bell's butler."

The prisoner, who was identified only as "Drake from North Sydney," was held in the Baddeck jail until his trial before Judge Dodd in June.

DR. JOHN L. BETHUNE,
C.1888

A doctor holds a special place in people's lives, providing care and guidance during life's most pivotal moments—whether delivering babies or delivering bad news.

Dr. John L. Bethune (1849–1913) attended to the health and welfare of the community in a variety of ways—as a justice of the peace, coroner, captain in the reserve militia, county warden, and politician in both the provincial and federal governments.

Born in 1849 in Loch Lomond, Richmond County, to Scottish immigrants, John's parents expected their son to become a minister. But he followed his heart, enrolling instead in medicine at Dalhousie University, and graduated in the second class to receive medical degrees at the Halifax institution.

He and his wife, Mary (Jones), had seven children, including Roderick and Clarence, both of whom went on to become doctors. Years later Dr. Clarence "Tabby" Bethune recalled peeking into the kitchen of the family home to watch his father perform surgery while his mother assisted. In an interview in the 1970s, Clarence remembered going with his father on a medical run north of Smokey to Meat Cove:

> I think it was 1912 because I was just old enough to remember. We left the wagon at the foot of Smokey and walked. Somebody met us with a sulky near the top. In order to pass another team we had to unhitch the horse and pull the sulkies around one another by hand as the road was so narrow. On that trip we stayed in a house at Meat Cove for about a week. They were very poor people. We had salt herring and potatoes three times a day and nothing else. At nighttime we slept on our carriage rug. I don't think my father ever got paid for that trip. I don't see where it could come from. More likely he gave money to the man.

In this photo of the main intersection in Baddeck, Dr. John L.
Bethune's home, MP John A. McDonald's home, and the peak of
the Telegraph House are visible on the left. On the right are Edward
McCurdy's store and the Baddeck Public Library.

It was summer resident George Kennan who gathered the Baddeck
townspeople together in September 1891 to suggest the creation of a
free public library. In a 1900 report, Kennan listed the following people as founding members of the Library Association for the Baddeck
Public Library: Mrs. S. G. A. McKeen, Georgina McCurdy, James
Dunlop, Margaret McPhee, Albert I. Hart, and H. Percy Blanchard,
appointed librarian. By the beginning of 1893, there were some four
hundred volumes of literature, including two sets of encyclopedias, on
the shelves in the library, which operated out of Sheriff James Dunlop's
courthouse office.

For such a small village, Baddeck's library also hosted an incredible array of accomplished speakers. In the 1890s Alexander Graham
Bell spoke about innovations in the new field of aviation. Major John
Wesley Powell, explorer of the Grand Canyon, spoke about his expedition. E. J. Glave, an associate of explorer H. M. Stanley, told a rapt
audience about his travels into the deepest wilds of Africa.

Alexander Graham and Mabel Bell were frequent contributors to the
library effort. In 1896 Mabel offered the use of Gertrude Hall as a library
and reading room. By 1900, the library was open every weekday from
October through April, with up to twenty visitors per night. Some 300
cardholders borrowed books over 2,500 times during that period.

A fire in December 1939 that destroyed three main street buildings also razed Gertrude Hall. Telegraph House owner Buddy Dunlop
recalled seeing a teenage Len Bethune rushing into the building and
carrying armloads of books into the cold December air. Others joined
Len, and some 1,800 books of the 7,000 housed there, were saved that
night.

John A. MacDonald (1851–1925) was a successful politician who happened to share his name with Canada's first prime minister. He won elections in Victoria County as both a Liberal and Conservative candidate. First elected in 1887 as a Conservative, MacDonald defeated Baddeck merchant and politician William F. McCurdy by just sixty votes. In a by-election later that same year, MacDonald went up against the formidable Charles J. Campbell, this time as a Liberal, and won by more than five hundred votes. He returned to the Tories for the next election in 1891 and defeated former Victoria MP William Ross before winning the seat by acclamation in 1892.

While campaigning in December 1891, MacDonald's home, which was located on the main street west of the Telegraph House, burned down. Alexander Graham Bell wrote the following to his wife regarding the fire:

> The house of John A. MacDonald—MP was burned down this morning between three and four o'clock. He was away on a canvassing tour. His wife and children had a narrow escape—saved in their night clothes. One of the children quite overcome by smoke, but all right now. Called on Mrs. MacDonald at Telegraph House and offered our sympathy. They have lost everything. Asked whether I could lend her anything from our house, but she replied that her friends in Baddeck had come forward to her assistance.

He was brash. He was bold. His fiery red hair matched his fiery hot temper. But Charles J. Campbell (1819–1906) had a gentle streak that surprised most people who came in contact with him.

He was an astute businessman and a tenacious politician. He oversaw the building of the *Highlander*, the first of forty ships he had built on Baddeck's waterfront. He served in the provincial legislature from 1871 and 1874. Between 1873 and 1887 he ran in seven elections, losing four and winning three, to serve as Victoria County's representative in Ottawa.

Campbell was born in the Isle of Skye in November 1819, the sixth of seven children born to Captain John Campbell and Isabella McRae. He was only a toddler when his father died in 1821. When his mother remarried almost a decade later, the couple immigrated to Nova Scotia with eleven-year-old Charles and his nine-year-old brother, Lauchlin. The Campbells' life in Inverness County was unsettled and his mother died at the hands of his stepfather.

Charles had an entrepreneurial spirit, and used his powerful connections to attract customers. When his cousin Sir Colin Campbell, the lieutenant-governor of Nova Scotia, visited, Charles insisted he park his royal carriage just outside the store.

In 1894, Campbell reminisced to Alexander Graham Bell about "Cape Breton before the steamboats and said for his part he preferred going up to Sydney in a boat built by the men of Barra with a good jug of rum beside him!" That same year, Mabel Bell went to see Campbell about borrowing some antiques for an exhibit. She described him as "that old reprobate that lives in the large square house on the hill opposite the post office and behind the hawthorn and lilac hedge." She added that she hadn't met him until that day, but that he "was so courtly in an old fashioned way" that she "took a great fancy to him. Mr. McCurdy (Arthur) says everyone feels the same way, though he is violent when under the influence of liquor that he has driven his whole family from him."

Campbell's face, etched in stone, continues to look out over Chebucto Street from above the main door at the Old Post Office.

BARCLAY TREMAIN,
c.1900

Lawyer Barclay Tremain (1839–1907) threw his hat into the political ring in the fall of 1874 and promptly found himself embroiled in controversy.

"Election all the topic of conversation, many candidates announced," Robert Elmsley wrote on nomination day, just two weeks before the vote for a seat in the House of Commons was to take place. Tremain, a Liberal, was running against Charles J. Campbell. A year earlier, Campbell had lost the federal election by just twenty votes to the Hon. William C. Ross, and this by-election was quickly becoming a repeat, with only eighteen votes separating Tremain and Campbell. After all the votes were counted and then recounted, Campbell was proclaimed the winner.

But not in Robert Elmsley's eyes. "CJC [Charles J. Campbell] declared elected member for Ottawa, in my opinion, illegally," he noted in his diary soon after the election.

On February 28, 1875, the Supreme Court of Nova Scotia overturned the election results. Barclay Tremain was declared the winner and went to Ottawa as the representative for Victoria County. He remained in office a total of 482 days, before resigning in August 1876 to accept a position as circuit judge for Baddeck, Sydney, and Arichat. Why the election was overturned was not noted, and Elmsley did not elaborate why he felt the original results were illegal. Charles Campbell won the next by-election held a month later by a hundred votes.

Before there was an official post office in Baddeck, the mail was sorted in a room in Robert Elmsley's home. On May 23, 1857, he wrote in his diary: "Postmaster. Salary nothing…but…allowed to frank letters [send mail for free] to the amount of three [ounces]."

In a May 1885 ad in the *Island Reporter*, Elmsley noted that mails for Halifax arrived daily at 9:00 A.M.; mail to Big Harbour, Big Baddeck, Margaree, and Middle River were delivered twice a week and "service hours [were] from 8:00 A.M.–7:00 P.M., Sunday excepted.

In the early 1880s Prime Minister John A. MacDonald launched a program to build post offices in communities with a population of ten thousand or more. Member of Parliament Charles J. Campbell used his influence to see that Baddeck was one of the communities chosen to have a Thomas Fuller-designed post office. (Fuller was the architect who designed the first Parliament Buildings in Ottawa.)

Elmsley kept track of each stage of the post office's construction in his diary:

> August 5, 1885 —first cargo stores came for post office
> August 24, 1885 —commenced digging foundation of post
>   office today
> August 25, 1885—men commenced dressing stone

Over the next fourteen months, stone by stone, the post office was built. On October 30, 1886, Elmsley was able to enter the building for the first time, although it sat empty until furniture arrived on December 19. With a northwest wind blowing on February 1, 1887, Elmsley noted that the steam boiler was operational. Three days later, as ice formed on the lake, the new post office opened for business.

VICTORIA COUNTY COUNCIL, C.1900

At the beginning of the twentieth century, this austere group of men governed the eighteen districts that made up Victoria County. Unfortunately, none of the men are identified in this photo. Since there are more than eighteen men in this photo, it is assumed that other courthouse employees also sat for the snapshot.

The following men were councillors in 1900–1901: John M. Buchanan (South Gut), Benjamin Dunlap (New Campbellton), Alexander MacDonald (Northside Little Narrows), Daniel MacDonald (Ingonish), Angus MacKay (Big Baddeck), Donald Mackenzie (Boularderie), Malcolm MacLean (Big Bras d'Or), Alex MacLeod (Englishtown), Donald B. MacLeod (North Shore), Farquhar MacRae (Middle River), Murdock D. McAskill (Baddeck), Charles McDonald (Bay St. Lawrence), Murdo McLeod (Cape North), Murdo G. Mcleod (Neils Harbour), Peter S. McLean (Washabuct), Neil McNeil (Iona), Malcolm McRitchie (North River), Malcolm McRitchie (North River), and Alexander W. Ross (south side Little Narrows).

Alex Taylor's house, located across the street from the first Baddeck Academy, can often be seen in the background of class photos.

Alex Taylor Jr. (1843–1928) was born in Beaverbank, near Halifax, in 1843. He was just a toddler when his Scottish immigrant parents arrived in the Baddeck area in 1847 and bought a piece of property on Baddeck Bay from William Kidston. Alex Sr. and Jr. both took active roles in the operation of the burgeoning community: Alex Sr. as *Custodes Rotulorum* ("keeper of the rolls," the equivalent of a country warden), and Alex Jr. as prothonotary (law clerk), county clerk, and registrar of deeds. In the 1930s, writer Alex MacLean recalled that Alex Taylor Jr. made a striking figure walking from his Shore Road home to the courthouse. Taylor apparently disliked the wooden sidewalks that lined Chebucto Street and refused to walk on them. Instead he strolled down the middle of the main street.

ROBERT JONES,
c.1865.

Robert Anderson Jones (1836–1866) was born in Big Baddeck, one of eight children of William Jones Jr. and Catherine Anderson. When he built a home on the corner of Chebucto and Twinning in 1860, he brought the Jones family from Big Baddeck to the village's main street. He married Janet Cameron in 1864 but was struck down by tuberculosis two years later at just thirty-one years old. His only child, Mary Catherine Jones, was still an infant.

Prior to his death, he was an early registrar of deeds for Victoria County. In the early twentieth century, his daughter, Mary, continued the family's civil service history, becoming registrar of deeds following the death of her husband Dr. John L. Bethune.

Samuel Cunard Campbell (1834–1911) grew up seeing ships wreck on the shores near his home on St. Paul Island. His father, John (?–1864), was appointed the first lightkeeper on the remote island located twenty-two kilometres (fourteen miles) off the coast of northern Cape Breton in 1838. St. Paul, with its jagged cliffs, lies at the entrance to the Gulf of St. Lawrence and has the unfortunate nickname Graveyard of the Gulf.

The waters around St. Paul Island were littered with the debris of hundreds of broken ships. The island, often shrouded in fog, halted vessels, tossing broken cargo and passengers into the freezing Atlantic. For the lucky few that managed to climb the steep rocks of the remote, barren island, there was little there to help them survive. As a result, government oversaw the construction of two lighthouses and a life-saving station in 1838.

By 1857, Sam, who was named after shipping magnate Samuel Cunard (a close associate of John Campbell and chairman of the lighthouse commissioners), had taken over from his father as superintendent of St. Paul Island. He administered the operations of the two lighthouses with their keepers (his brother, Norman Campbell, and Dougall McKay) and a crew of men trained in various life-saving techniques, including how to launch rowboats into the rough seas. His annual salary in 1857 was one hundred pounds.

In October 1873, Sam married Margaret Mckenzie Archibald, of Gleneg, Guysborough County. John Malcolm, the oldest of their five children, was known as "Johnny Sam," and he followed in his father and grandfather's footsteps to become superintendent of St. Paul Island from 1891 to 1920. He was also MLA for Victoria County from 1937 to 1949. Johnny Sam's four daughters, Jessie (1879–?), Jean (1881–1960), Lena (1886–1968), and Ethel (1889–?) were all born on the island. The Campbells split their time between St. Paul and Baddeck, where they lived in a home on Bay Road, a kilometre past the Bay Pond.

This, the second courthouse built in Baddeck, was opened in 1889. The first Baddeck Courthouse (and jail) was built in the same location in 1856 at a cost of six hundred pounds sterling. William Kidston donated the land near the centre of Chebucto Street for the building.

The photo shows the west side of the courthouse and details that are no longer visible since a wing was added in 1967. The fire of 1926 began in the buildings on the right (slightly obscured by the telegraph pole).

Francis McGreggor (1882–1968), an oft-kilted Victoria County resident and author, described a typical nomination day in his book *Days that I Remember.*

> Nomination day would be held a week or ten days previous to the date of the election and all the parties would meet in Baddeck. Each candidate would speak alternately for an hour with a short rebuttal from the balcony above the door at the courthouse. The public would gather on the grass below and heckling was common and sometimes it was difficult for the politicians to answer some of the questions put to them by the witty wags. Often fights would break out in the streets. Consequently, Nomination Day in Baddeck was full of excitement.

Charles McCurdy (1879–1957) had a keen sense of history. He understood that momentous occasions, like his cousin J. A. D. McCurdy's first flight in Canada, had secured Baddeck's place in history. But he also understood that history is found in the ordinary and day-to-day.

McCurdy served as county clerk treasurer from 1922 to 1955. As treasurer, he presented an annual report to council. He began his 1945 address by stating: "We are now in the sixth year of the Great War… now 808 of our young people in the Armed Forces are from Victoria County."

Included in the dry figures of the 1940 cash disbursements were payments of $6,675.00 to the department of highways, $49.88 for repairs to the courthouse, and $55.00 for the now-forgotten practice of "bushing the ice"—laying trees along the frozen Bras d'Or Lake to make temporary roadway markings on the ice.

In September 1926, as homes and businesses at the east end of the main street of Baddeck went up in flames, Charles left the rescue effort at his own home and rushed into the courthouse to save minute books, registry ledgers, and account records. Many of the books he saved that morning make up part of the Victoria County Archives today.

ROYAL BANK, 1956   A bank has existed at the corner of Chebucto and Prince streets for over one hundred years. In August 1902 the Union Bank of Halifax opened a branch in Baddeck in this building, which was formerly the Albert I. Hart mercantile and general store. In 1910, the Royal Bank, then Canada's third largest bank, bought the Union Bank's assets and its thirty-seven branches across Nova Scotia, including the Baddeck branch.

The Royal Bank operated at this location until 1964, when it was demolished to make way for a modern one-storey brick building. The bank managers who oversaw Baddeck's finances from this building include: R. W. Elliott (1902–1903); W. R. Wright (1903–1904); J. J. Lyons (1904–1907); J. A. Irving (1907–1911); H. W. Smith (1911–1912); J. H. McDaniel (1912–1913); R. T. Moseley (1913–1915); F. C.Dickie (1915–1919); H. G. Bowes (1919–1922); R. S. Hopgood (1922–1925); C. M. V. Spence (1925–1928); H. L. Hall (1928–1954); J. F. Forbes (1954–1962); D. S. McLeod (1962–1963); and G. A. Miller, who was manager from 1963–1966 and presided over both buildings.

Chapter 7

The Waterfront and Principal Streets

TREMAIN HOUSE, C.1880

In this image, Barclay Tremain stands with two of his daughters before his home on Chebucto Street. The stately two-storey home, built about 1867, was located near the east end of the present site of the Victoria County Memorial Hospital.

CAROLINE (OLD) TREMAIN, c.1880

Within a few months of Barclay Tremain's arrival in Baddeck in 1861, his name appears in Robert Elmsley's diary. (Indeed, Tremain was a regular feature in Elmsley's periodic weigh-ins of local residents, and he tipped the scales at 261 pounds.) The ever-curious postmaster noted that Tremain and his "lady arrived on the Banshee from Halifax married." Tragically, within a year, the young Kate (Shields) Tremain died in childbirth with the couple's first child.

Tremain's second wife was Caroline Old, the daughter of George Old, a master shipbuilder from Boularderie, who coincidentally had built the steamer Banshee in 1851. Caroline (Old) and Barclay Tremain raised eleven children in the large and elaborately decorated house and hosted many formal soirees there. Alexander Graham Bell notes in a letter to his wife in 1891 that he had Christmas dinner at the Tremains' home.

In the 1940s the home was purchased by businessman George P. Fraser and renovated for use by the Baddeck Rotary Club. The upstairs housed the Baddeck Public Library. By the 1970s it contained a number of apartments. It was torn down in the early 1990s.

In this photo, the western tip of Kidston Island is visible on the left, with the hills of Washabuct in the background.

Sam McKnight, a nephew of William Kidston Sr., visited William and Margaret (Duffus) Kidston in 1877. By this time, only a barn and a couple of roaming heifers remained on the island. The Kidston home and store was located just outside the frame of this photo.

McKnight described the area in an 1877 letter:

> The house is built right on the bank of the lake with a road only between. The ground that it and the neighbouring houses occupy may be called a peninsula as there is a stagnant pool on one side and a bay on the other. The form of the shore caused by this bay give it the name of the 'The Point.' On the other side of the bay is a projection which seems to deserve the name better. It is called graveyard point, because in the early days of the village it was used as the burying place. The old Lady's three Duffus children lie there….The old lady (Margaret Duffus Kidston) holds the island a particularly valuable possession. She had her dwelling house there when she first came to the place, during her former husband's lifetime. No traces of a house are there, though besides the aforementioned barn, there is an old apple tree, which once fell down in a storm and was set up again and yielded fruit.

McCurdy's Lane was a short road that linked the waterfront to
the main street. Before 1888, the building at the top of the lane
was McCurdy and Sons General Store; at the base of the lane was
McCurdy's Wharf. By the mid-1890s, the store was McKay, McAskill
and Company, and the dock was known as Steamship Wharf.

   The building on the left is referred to as The Ark, and the yard
on the right is Mother Gaelic's, on the corner of McCurdy's Lane and
Water Street.

An image similar to this one appeared in an 1895 edition of *Outlook* magazine, an American periodical published at the turn of the twentieth century, and is credited to photographer William Watson.

Spectacle Island, two gentle knolls rising just behind Kidston Island, was named for its similarity to the shape of eyeglasses. In the century since the photo was taken, Spectacle Island has become two completely separate islands; together, they more closely resemble an exclamation point.

In the 1970s, with scrawny defoliated trees standing at one end, Spectacle Island was colloquially called Toothbrush Island. In the mid-1990s the provincial government declared the two dots of land on both islands and the waters around them a bird sanctuary.

The Loch Bhreagh House has been a silent witness to 150 years of history. In 1853, when Ewen Campbell built the inn, fewer than fifty people lived in Baddeck. Knox Church (on the Bay Road) was not even a decade old; Alexander Graham Bell, the area's most famous resident, was just six years old.

When Catherine Dunlop, future proprietress of the Telegraph House, first arrived in Baddeck, she stayed at Campbell's Inn. From there she watched the busy waterfront and recognized the potential of the tiny community.

By the time Benjamin Hoppin, a New England writer and explorer, took possession of the house he renamed Loch Bhreagh in 1893, the little church built by pioneers on the Bay Road had relocated to the centre of Baddeck. Catherine Dunlop's Telegraph House was a vibrant operation heading into its thirty-third year, and the population of the village was about 1,800 people. By then, Baddeck was frequently a topic of conversation in North American newspapers and magazines, as telephone inventor Alexander Graham and Mabel Bell had just completed their thirty-seven room mansion, Beinn Bhreagh Hall.

People relax on the step at the home of Millionaire McNeil, on Shore Road. Today this home is part of the main reception building of the Inverary Inn.

Neil McNeil (1842–1921) returned to Victoria County from Massachusetts in the late 1880s after having made his fortune as a building contractor in the Boston states. When he began building large homes in Baddeck for his relatives, he earned the nickname "Millionaire McNeil."

McNeil built three landmark houses still in use in the twenty-first century: the main houses at both the Inverary Inn and Gisele's Inn, as well as the McNeil House at the Silver Dart Lodge. Each was built in the same style, with a peaked roof and a distinctive decorative design in the point. Each house also had a stunning view of the Bras d'Or and McNeil's birthplace of Washabuct.

In August 1898, the *Baddeck Telephone* newspaper noted "the arrival of Neil McNeil Esq. of Boston on Saturday last to spend some time at his summer residence. Besides doing much to beautify the town architecturally and otherwise, Mr. McNeil takes a great interest in local industry. He is one of Cape Breton's energetic and successful sons."

McNeil never married. Following his death in 1921, his estate was divided among seventeen of his nieces and nephews, and all of his automobiles, robes, and the contents of two Massachusetts homes were left to St. Francis Xavier University in Antigonish.

In this photo Dr. Bethune's house is on the far left, Greenwood Manse is in the middle, and Thomas McLean's home is on the right.

The first McLean residence at this location burned overnight on July 10, 1886. That same night, Mabel Bell, who was then staying at the Telegraph House (to the east of Dr. Bethune's and outside the frame of the photo), noted that a bright orange light stirred her while she slept. She thought it may have been the sun rising, but upon awakening, realized the light was coming from the west. It was the fire at McLean's that had awakened her.

The McLean family were educators. Father Thomas (T. S.) was a principal at Baddeck Academy. His daughters, Christina (1874–1953) and Agnes (1884–?), taught there as well, and Christina even followed in her father's footsteps, serving as principal before retiring in 1937. Neither Christina nor Agnes married, and the two lived together in the rebuilt family home after their retirements. They were collectively known as "Tena and Aggie-O."

A report that the sisters had arrived in the village for the summer appeared in the July 1927 edition of the *Victoria News*: "Miss Tina O. McLean, principal of the Annapolis Royal Academy and Miss S. Agnes McLean of the Glace Bay school staff are occupying the Baddeck residence for the summer."

How did these children stay clean beside such a muddy road? The answer to that question is lost to history, as are the children's names. They are sitting next to Taylor's Pond, the body of water now commonly called the Bay Pond, located just below the Alexander Graham Bell National Historic Site. In the background near the shoreline are a Mi'kmaq encampment and a hayfield that later became the driveway to the Bell Museum.

In her unpublished manuscript, "Some Early Baddeckers: A genealogy of the Sparlings and Elmsleys," author Florence Sparling describes early curling matches on the pond:

> The curling stones were brought from Scotland by the older generation and used by the youngsters as soon as they were old enough to lift them. At the age of eleven or twelve, Karl [son of Emily Elmsley and Leaver Sparling] recalled taking the stones on a sled from his house to the pond. The stones had the long iron handle and the game was played by releasing the stone from the hack....The ice surface varied, slanting in one direction, then another, now shell ice, now smooth. The curling game came to an end when the stones were left on the ice and a thaw came, leaving the stones on the bottom of the pond.

ABOVE

MASONIC HALL (AT
LEFT), C.1900

TOP OF PAGE

VIEW OF GRANT STREET
FROM MASONIC HALL,
C.1900

In 1875, master masons Archibald Kidston, John MacDonald, and Neil Mackenzie purchased a lot of land from William Kidston Sr., Archibald's father, for one hundred dollars. The land was within the village, and the three men purchased it for the express purpose of building a Masonic Lodge. Where the lodge members met prior to 1875 is not clear, but one early map of the village notes a lodge near present-day Campbell Street. When the lodge built at the corner of Grant and Queen streets was destroyed by fire in 1898, Mabel Bell offered the Masons a $1,500 mortgage, which was paid in full a dozen years later. Although owned by St. Mark's Masonic Order, the hall frequently hosted public activities. In 1899, the Young Ladies Club of Baddeck organized a highly successful flower show there. The hall also hosted plays and art shows and was used as a movie house for several generations of Baddeck teens.

The July 13, 1898, edition of the *Baddeck Telephone* reported on the progress of the rebuilding effort: "Work on the new Masonic temple is going ahead full swing. The building is being erected on the site of the old hall destroyed by fire a year ago. The plans promise a fine modern structure which will reflect credit upon the energy and pluck of the Masonic fraternity and will be used as a town hall much needed."

The wooden boardwalk that extends down the southern side of Chebucto Street was a project of the Young Ladies Club of Baddeck. The meetings of the educational and social club were held in members' homes, where ladies would gather in parlours to learn about such diverse subjects as the need for good roads and life in Russia. With the wooden sidewalk, the hems of the women's dresses were not dragged through the muck of the streets before entering members' homes for the biweekly meetings. In this photo of Baddeck's main street, the Telegraph House rises on the left. In the distance, a horse is tied to a hitching post near the front of the courthouse. The tall square White Store can be seen on the right.

R. T. Vooght, one of the Vooght brothers who operated a large three-storey department store in North Sydney, operated a small branch shop in Baddeck. This ad, found under the heading "Local and General" in the August 9, 1899, edition of the *Baddeck Telephone*, illustrates the tools available for purchase.

> "Just received: scythes, rakes, stones, machine oil, whips, washboards and brooms. ~ R. T. Vooght.

VIEW OF BADDECK FROM STEAMER, 1907

The following appeared in the *Baddeck Telephone* newspaper on July 13, 1899:

> The port of Baddeck has been enlivened of late by the arrival at and departure from our piers of several steamers, sailing vessels and numerous small craft. The schooner 'Soudan' with Captain McFarlane arrived from Boston recently loaded with flour and meal. The captain formerly belonged to Margaree and for some time sailed from this port in the Newfoundland trade. The schooner 'Satelite' commanded by Capt. John A. McKenzie, sailed from Baddeck on Monday the 4th for St. Pierre, with a general cargo comprising cattle, sheep, hay, etc. Also wharf logs, spars, etc. There is more 'get-up' to the square inch in Capt. John than in any man we know. We wish our old friend success in his new venture.

Left to right: Charlie Fraser, Clarence "Tabby" Bethune, Ethel Fraser, Norman Bethune Sr., Janet Bethune, Dr. John L. Bethune.

Dr. John L. Bethune stands at the front of his home and office at the corner of Chebucto and Twining streets; the annex to the left is his office. By the time this photo was snapped, Dr. Bethune's oldest son, Robert, was twenty-four; his youngest was only three. This photo was in an album compiled by Norman Bethune Sr. In later years he told his grandchildren about his four brothers and one sister: "It was a big family, five boys and a sister for each of us."

From this corner one gets a sense of the ebb and flow of life in Baddeck. When Robert Jones (grandfather to Clarence and Janet) built this house about 1860, Chebucto Street had recently been carved from the hillside and declared the village's main thoroughfare. By the mid-1880s the door to Dr. John L. Bethune's busy office opened to Twinning Street, the former footpath that connected the settlement at Big Baddeck to Duffus's island store in the 1840s. Across the street was the junction of Shore Road and the road to the Margarees, where farmers carted wagon loads of produce into the village. In this photo, Dr. John L.'s two youngest children stand on the front step of their home at Bethune's Corner in the spring of 1908, with the peak of the Telegraph House and the White Store in the background.

Active sailing seasons began at the Bras d'Or Yacht Club in 1904, just after the club was formed, even though an official clubhouse wasn't built until 1912. In July 1907, J. A. D. McCurdy was the master of ceremonies as flags that signalled the start and finish of each race were raised on the specially built flagstaff beside the lighthouse at Kidston's Island. In 1910, an illuminated motorboat parade was held during the first week of August. Each of the boats was decorated with multi-coloured candle lanterns and sailed from Kidston's Island down the bay, past the homes on the Beinn Bhreagh estate. The parade was written up in the *Beinn Bhreagh Recorder*:

> The evening being fine, both calm and dark, quite a large number of boats turned out. The Commodore of the Club, Mr. J. A. Irving, in Mr. Peary's motor boat *Tam II* took the lead, followed by Capt. Peter McFarlane. Capt. McFarlane had in tow Mr. G. H. Grosvenor's boat the *Alexander* and several row boats. Following were *Edruma, Hope, Shamrock, Aberdare, Rose, Comet* and a great number of other motor boats...some of these towed as many as five row boats.

The air inside Gertrude Hall could be humid, especially during the hazy days of summer. In July 1904 many of the sailors in the hall were likely daydreaming of being out on the lake, with a warm breeze chasing them into hidden coves, but there were important details to attend to first. Charles Carruth had called a dozen sailing enthusiasts together to consider forming a yacht club.

With its relatively protected waters, little fog, and countless sheltered harbours to explore, the Bras d'Or was a sailor's paradise. As the village entered the twentieth century, the once booming shipbuilding industry had dwindled, and sailing was becoming a recreational sport.

Schooners often raced between Kidston Island and Washabuct, using a pennant-draped flagpole near the lighthouse as the starting point.

As the meeting convened on that July day, all present quickly agreed that a club should be formed. The minutes of the first meeting, as recorded by Arthur W. McCurdy, read: "Those present considering themselves organized as a club (and) themselves as charter members." A decision to call the club the Baddeck Yacht Club brought about much discussion, but in the end, the group decided to honour the lake, and the Bras d'Or Yacht Club was born. Admission to join was set at fifty cents, and annual dues were the same.

While the club members began planning races within days of the inaugural meeting, a clubhouse wasn't built on the waterfront for another decade. The charter members of the Bras d'Or Yacht Club were: Charles Carruth, William Arnold, John E. Campbell, Dan A. McRae, George F. McRae, H. Percy Blanchard, P. L. McFarlane, Arthur McCurdy, Dr. D. A. McIver, George Hollifield, George McKay, and Gilbert Grosvenor.

ANNUAL REGATTA, c.1939

Regatta Week at the Bras d'Or Yacht Club was, and still is, a celebration of the art and science of sailing. Since the club's earliest days, the first week in August has always brought a multitude of sailboats to the village. Sailors from North Sydney, Sydney, the mainland, and beyond brought their experience and love for the sport to Baddeck for race week. A Sunday afternoon sail-past, for years led by the brown-sailed *Elsie,* marked the beginning of the summer celebration and was eagerly anticipated by spectators lining the shores along Water Street and Baddeck Bay Road.

Although construction for the customs house and post office began in 1885, Baddeck had postal service as early as 1840. At that time, Thomas Battersly would arrive once a week from Sydney, on foot and "with a bag slung on his back…sometimes one letter or a paper" inside, wrote Robert Elmsley.

Baddeck's postmasters included: Joseph Campbell (1840s); William Kidston (1852); Robert Elmsley (1868–1893); Mary McLean (1894–1896); Tina C. McLean (1896–1898); Donald J. McRae (1898–1908); Bessie McRae (1908–1911); James B. Fraser (1911–1950); Murdock Matheson (1949–1953); Mary MacPhail (1953). Alton Langille (1953–1973) was the last postmaster to oversee the mails from the corner of Jones and Chebucto streets.

In the early days of the last century, the members of the municipal council of Victoria County grappled with the issue of how to regulate motor cars as they travelled the county's roads.

Horse-drawn wagons came face to face with the newfangled horse-less carriages on the narrow streets and twisting roads. The tires on the cars carved new tracks, making travel by wagons and covered carriages difficult for horse and rider.

In September 1909, the *Victoria News* mentioned the first time a motor car wheeled through the nearby community of Estmere, forty-eight kilometres west of Baddeck: "A party from Sydney with an automobile passed through here this week, the first ever seen in this place. With the exception of frightening a few horses we have heard of no damage done by the machine."

In January 1910, the council set out the following regulations:

> Motor Cars can be driven on public highways on Tuesdays, Wednesdays and Thursdays only.
> Speed limit: maximum 10 miles per hour.
> Motor Cars must stop when approached by a horse-drawn vehicle and remain stopped until it passes.
> Any violators will be fined up to $20 for a first offense; up to $50 for a second offense or 30 days in jail, or both. For a third offense, fine up to $100 or 60 days in jail, or both.

In this photo Casey Baldwin leans on his 1919 Dodge, while the man with him appears to be holding up a baseball glove. The men and cars are in front of the The Ark, a well-travelled building. Originally built in Washabuct on the shore opposite Baddeck, The Ark was floated across the lake around 1898. The house was owned by a man named McLean. Once the house and its owner were settled in Baddeck, both were renamed. The building became The Ark, and its owner was nicknamed Noah.

Between the cars is a blacksmith shop, once operated by the MacDonald Brothers. Located near the corner of Cameron and Water streets, the Ark and the blacksmith shop were unassuming greeters to passengers as they disembarked at Steamship Wharf.

LYNWOOD, C.1900

Merchant Charles Hart built this large and elaborate home around 1879. He was the son of Joseph and Maria (Ingraham) of Margaree. Charles, with his younger brother, Albert Irad, operated a mercantile on the corner of Chebucto and Prince streets from 1880–1902. A. H. Sutherland, a director with the Bras d'Or Steamship Company, purchased the house sometime around 1900. Sutherland accompanied Benjamin Hoppin on a trek to the Arctic in 1896. His daughter, Edith Sutherland, spent almost forty years in Korea with her husband, Duncan "Korea" MacRae, a missionary.

For years, the large front yard boasted an extensive orchard, and school kids often visited, nabbing an apple on their way to school. By the middle half of the twentieth century, the house featured a gift shop and art gallery and operated under the name Lynwood. Since the early 1990s it has been an inn.

BROADWATER,
c.1890

From the home called Broadwater on Baddeck Bay, Ohio native George Kennan explored Baddeck's flora and fauna. Kennan, an associate of the Bell Family, was an author, explorer, and noted expert on Russia. He arrived in Baddeck shortly after the Bells discovered the area in the mid-1880s.

Alexander Graham Bell described the property to Kennan at a dinner party the two men were attending in Washington, D.C. According to writer Lilas Toward, by the time the party was over, Kennan had contacted owner Caroline Anderson and bought the property sight unseen.

The land the home was built on was first deeded to shipping magnate Samuel Cunard, brother-in-law of James Duffus, the merchant who first settled on Kidston Island. It is possible that Cunard built a house on the property that was incorporated into the house that followed.

Kennan, along with thirty other men, was one of the founders of the National Geographic Society in 1888. The other founders included Alexander Graham Bell's father-in-law, Gardiner Greene Hubbard, and explorers Adolphus Greely and Wesley Powell.

Chapter 8

Snapshots of Village Life

A WOMAN AT ALEXANDER TAYLOR'S SHORE ROAD HOME, C.1900

With the advent of the Kodak Brownie in 1900, the art of photography was put in the hands of the people. George Eastman's developments—using film instead of cumbersome glass plates and chemicals—allowed everyday people to take informal snapshots of their surroundings. No longer was photography simply stuffy portraiture. Instead it could be used to record friends gathered on the step on a nice spring day, a baseball team's success, or a sail on the lake—snapshots of moments that remain enduring views into the past.

These decorative garlands were strung over the main street to greet
Lord Aberdeen, the governor general of Canada, and his wife, Lady
Ishabel, when they visited Baddeck in 1897. Their visit coincided with
a deluge of rain that made for muddy travelling between the town,
where the Aberdeens spoke at the courthouse, and Beinn Bhreagh,
where the Bells hosted a dinner in their honour.

"It was the greatest shame though that it was pouring hard all
the time they were here and so spoilt the effect of the hard work the
townspeople bestowed on decorating Baddeck," Mabel Bell wrote in a
letter to her daughter, Daisy, after the Aberdeens' visit.

The garlands were strung at various businesses along the main
street. This one, across Chebucto near the McKay and Company store,
offered "Greetings" to the dignitaries as they entered the village.

94TH BATTALION DURING DRILLS AT CAMP IN BIG BADDECK, C.1898

"Sons of the Argyle Highlanders" was composed while the 94th Battalion of the Argyle Highlanders was encamped along the Baddeck River. The lyrics appeared in a July 1898 edition of the *Baddeck Telephone*. Commander Lieutenant Colonel John L. Bethune issued a challenge for a composer to create a fitting melody.

"Sons of the Argyle Highlanders"
by Jas. D. Irving

Sons of the mountainland, stems of the heather
Hark to the bugle, as it rings through the glen!
Stirs not each soul with the wildest emotion
Lives not the memory of Old Scotland again?
Stern land of our fathers, though far from the shore.
Dear to thy hearts are thy memories grand
Still through our veins run the blood of thy heroes
Oh! Who would not die for our glorious land?

Chorus: Proudly then proudly, Argyle to the front
Sound the wild pibroch through the vales of Bras d'Or

Stir the wild blood of each hardy young Isleman
Donald and Roderick and Malcolm Canmore
See the proud emblem that tells of our birth
Floating in grandeur in yon quiet vale.
Under its folds, we enjoy every blessing
Glory and honour that none can assail
Gather, then gather, ye sons of Cape Breton
True to the land that our forefathers gave us
Canada's boast! To our Queen we are loyal,
Britons, we are ever 'Dileas do'n Bhrataich.'

Chorus

Sons of the mountainland descendants of heroes
March then as marched our forefathers of yore
Rise the wild slogan cry 'Scotland forever!'
Til it rings through the vales of bonny Bras d'Or.
Shoulder to shoulder lads, step it out bravely,
Men from the intervale, mountain and glen,
Dileas Do'n Bhrataich* raise the wild call again
Britons proud are we and soldiers of the Queen.

Chorus

*Dileas Do'n Bhrataich means "True to the Flag," and was the motto of the 94th Battalion.

94TH HIGHLANDERS MILITARY BAND, 1898

On warm summer evenings at the turn of the last century, sweeping waltzes and driving marches would drift over the village, as the 94th Highlanders Military Band performed outdoor concerts. A bandstand, located near the intersection of Shore Road, Chebucto Street, and the road to Margaree, was their usual stage, but they also hosted concerts at the Masonic Hall, where a typical program would include waltzes composed by Caroline Lowthian and marches by Mills. Lawyer Percy Blanchard first organized the band in 1893. The band's instruments were stored at the MacKay, McAskill store and were lost in the September 1926 fire.

Among those in the photo are: Malcolm McLeod, Harvey Rice, D. N. McDonald, Dan Ferguson, M. J. Morrison, bandleader George Hollifield, A. N. Mckenzie, W. R. Ferguson, Murdo Carmichael, John Amireault, Duncan Ferguson, Archie McDonald, Dave Dunlop, George Payne, and J. MacKenzie.

**BOY ON BAY ROAD,
c.1898**

This photo shows the entrance to Baddeck as it looked at the turn of the twentieth century. Behind the boy is the Bay Pond, which was known as Taylors Pond in 1898, as Alexander Taylor Sr. had a house to the east of it. The dusty Bay Road twists and turns to become Chebucto Street, the village's main thoroughfare, where the square, flat roof of the McKay, McAskill and Company store can be seen on the right. Behind it, the two chimneys of Duntulum House, the elaborate home of Charles J. Campbell, are visible, as is the spire of Greenwood Church.

The driveway to the Alexander Graham Bell National Historic Site now winds up the hill on the opposite shore of the pond. Before the museum was built, undertaker Charles McAskill's hayfield and barn, where he stored his horse-drawn hearse, were located here.

Emily Taylor and two unidentified people (and a dog) stand with oars
at the Exhibition Grounds beside the Baddeck Academy. The man
may be Emily's future husband, Pierce Mecutchen, a Philadelphia lawyer. The two married on December 27, 1904, in Baddeck. At Taylor's
Shore Road home in the background, someone stands at the gate, waiting.

To mark the thirtieth anniversary of the Young Ladies Club of
Baddeck (later the Alexander Graham Bell Club), members who lived
outside Baddeck were asked to write letters about their recollections of
their time spent in the club. In 1921, Emily, who had been living in
Philadelphia for seventeen years by that time, recalled:

> As a child I remember how much I enjoyed the girls
> [sewing] club which met at her house [Mrs. Bell's home,
> Beinn Bhreagh] every Saturday morning. When I was
> making Edward's [her son] baby clothes I thought of Mrs.
> Bell so much and that only for her I would never have been
> able to make them at all. I am quite proud to add that my
> nurse said she had had a good many baby cases but never
> one where the baby had such beautiful clothes as mine—all
> hand made.

ON TAYLOR'S STEP,
c.1900

This picture was found in one of Norman Bethune Sr.'s many photo albums, but unlike other snapshots in his care, this photo lacked identification. The house (visible in the background of a school photo) was recognized as Alexander Taylor's Shore Road home, located across from Baddeck Academy.

Though some information about the photo is now known, many questions remain. Why are these women gathered together? What is the air of joviality, the thread of connection among them? The front door behind them is open, adding to the scene's casual nature. The older woman and the youngest girl are holding hands. Are they grandmother and granddaughter?

Identified in the photo are: *bottom left*, Emily (Taylor) Mecutchen; *middle left*, unknown, but possibly Jessie Campbell, daughter of Sam Cunard and Margaret Archibald; *seated on bottom stair*, unknown, but may be Jessie Campbell's sister, Lena; *seated on top stair*, Mrs. Alexander Taylor Sr.; *seated on railing*, Janie (Taylor) Burke; standing at bottom right, Mrs. Alexander Taylor Jr.

THE NEVER SWETS, MAY 24, 1908

In the summer of 1908, the *Sydney Daily Post* carried reports of both cricket and baseball matches played in Sydney, North Sydney, and Glace Bay. The game likely had an enthusiastic fan in Frederick "Casey" Baldwin, whose nickname was bestowed upon him because of his baseball skill as a boy in Ontario (Casey recalling the famous poem, "Casey at the Bat"). He arrived in Baddeck two years before these teams played this championship game on May 24, 1908, when the Never Swets won the trophy.

Members of the team were, *back row, left to right:* John McLeod; Dan McNeil; Ian McDonald; Neil McDonald (captain); Neil McNeil; Gerald Dunlop; Sam McDonald (umpire). *Front row, left to right:* Bob McDonald; Gordon Bethune; William McLean.

DIRTY SHIRTS, MAY 24, 1908

The Dirty Shirts pose after losing to the Never Swets in the championship game.

In the coming years, a number of the boys from the Never Swets and the Dirty Shirts matured into local businessmen, doctors, and one celebrated journalist. Gerald Dunlop, grandson of the first proprietors of the Telegraph House, took over the operation. His brother Graham became an electrician in Sydney. Neil McNeil went from being the Washabuct correspondent for the *Victoria News* in Baddeck to the staff of the *New York Times*, where he became managing editor before retiring in 1951. Others fought overseas in World War I, including Ian MacDonald, Jack MacKenzie, and Ben Blanchard, the son of lawyer Percy Blanchard. Roddie Bethune became a medical officer, serving overseas in both world wars. William McAskill, whose father was part owner of the McKay, McAskill and Company store, was killed in action in France in 1917.

Members of the Dirty Shirts were, *front row, left to right*: Stanley McDonald (referee); Ben Blanchard; Roddie Bethune; Fred McLennan (captain); Robert Bethune; William McAskill; Jack McKenzie. *Back row, left to right*: Graham Dunlop; Johnie McKay.

After forty-three years, the 94th Victoria Regiment, formed in 1871, was placed on active service.

The men of the battalion provided protection along the Cape Breton seacoast, but many in the 94th were also recruited into two battalions—the 85th Nova Scotia Highlanders and the 185th Cape Breton Highlanders—that went overseas. Many of these men fought in France, some at Vimy Ridge.

Like so many of his comrades, Francis McGreggor of Nyanza shipped out in the spring of 1915, landing in Britain on June 1. His battalion was absorbed into the British Army. This excerpt is taken from McGreggor's biography, which he presented to the Alexander Graham Bell Club in 1961:

> The road along into Belgium was strewn with extra stuff that the boys threw away to lighten their packs...The sounds of guns up ahead grew louder by the hour, a grim reminder of what lay ahead. We marched fifty minutes of every hour, ten minutes rest and off again. The pipes and drums played ten minutes and carried their instruments ten minutes. This was the last long march for many of those boys that I came to know...It rained all that fall and winter. We had no protection from it. The trenches became filled with dirty, stinking water. The British dead lay unburied.

Rations consisted of bully-beef, hard tack and a bottle of water. Dry tea was issued and tommy-cookers, a small can of stuff that could boil a little water. The old tea leaves were saved and boiled over and over. No milk, butter, sugar or any change until we were relieved in about two weeks time. In those days we had no labour battalion so that our relief was not a rest. All night we had to serve as carrying parties, bringing ammunition, trench stores and rations to our comrades in the line. Their turn would come when we went in again....Only the few that remain now in the autumn of life, can remember the horrors of those early days of war.

As the casualties piled up at Vimy Ridge in April 1917, it was the 85th Highlanders—charged with trench digging—who suddenly found themselves storming the all-important Hill 145. Major Percival Anderson, a farmer from Big Baddeck, and his D Company were first over the hill. Anderson was awarded the Military Cross for his "dauntless courage." He was killed in action six months later at Passchendaele.

AT A BASEBALL GAME, 1912

This crew of baseball players is taking a time out while the game goes on behind them. The game may have taken place at Beinn Bhreagh, as the hilly background bears some resemblance to the grounds near the lodge. *Front row, left to right*: Graham Dunlop, Gordon Bethune, Donnie McPherson, Bob MacDonald, Bennie McAskill. *Back row, left to right*: unknown, Dan Alan McNeil.

Baddeck residents played a variety of sports in the early twentieth century, including curling, hockey, baseball, and quoits, a lawn game similar to horseshoes. Beinn Bhreagh laboratory workers issued good-natured challenges to Baddeck men to partake in both winter and summer sports.

In March 1909, the Beinn Bhreagh *Recorder* noted that after flying over the frozen lake for much of the day, pilot J. A. D. McCurdy "finished off the afternoon by taking part in a vigorous game of hockey on the ice (Beinn Bhreagh Laboratory vs. Baddeck) and helped to win the game."

That same winter, the *Recorder* also carried information about teams playing the old Scottish national game of curling on the frozen Bras d'Or Lakes. Casey Baldwin donated a cup that was awarded to the team that garnered the most points during the 1908–1909 season (that year, it was won by Baldwin's Beinn Bhreagh team).

This mischievous group is hamming it up for the camera. *Back row, left to right*: Norman Bethune Sr., Charlie Moffatt, Robbie Watson; *middle row*: Roach MacLean, Mr. Grainger, Mack MacAulay, Maurice Watson; *front row*: Chester MacKay, unidentified.

This photo may have been taken at the MacDonald Brother's machine shop, located on the waterfront near the present-day Baddeck Marine Wharf. Prior to opening the shop, Sam MacDonald was a photographer for Alexander Graham Bell at Beinn Breagh, and his brother Bob was an engineer on the mail boats.

The steamship *Marion* was arguably the finest vessel of the Bras d'Or steamer fleet. Outfitted with a saloon, large staterooms, and a dining room, it carried passengers and freight between Bras d'Or Lake ports and Sydney. Before arriving in Cape Breton in the early 1880s, the *Marion* was an excursion boat on the Hudson River, plying the same upstate New York waters once traversed by Jonathan Jones, Baddeck's earliest settler.

Few clues remain about these Marion passengers. They may have come from a Young Ladies Club afternoon picnic to Washabuct, where they might have picked wildflowers and arranged them into fanciful designs on their hats. Or perhaps these women have just come from a more solemn gathering, as they all appear to be dressed in black. Is the spectacle-wearing woman, with her arms sternly placed on her hips, admonishing the unseen photographer for snapping her photo on such an occasion?

**TWO HATS AND A BOW,
C.1913**

Florrie J. P. McLeod (back left), sister of merchant J. P. McLeod; Dorothy Crowdis (back right), daughter of Henry and Annie Crowdis of Big Baddeck; and Jean McDougall (front), daughter of Rev. Donald McDougall, minister of Greenwood church.

What grand occasion these three ladies are dressed for is unknown. At the turn of the last century, hats were an essential part of every woman's wardrobe, and the latest styles of the new season were always launched at Easter. Summer hats were crafted from braided straw, and decorated with taffeta, silk, or satin. Accents were often opulent—peacock plumes, ribbons, or lace, and for the truly daring, artificial birds or fruit.

If no hat was worn, then special occasions were marked with a sweeping updo hairstyle, with a large bow attached at the back of the head.

Nicknames are not unique to Baddeck, but there have been a few great ones christened in the town. Fred MacDonald was known as Freddie Phone because he ran the telephone office; Angus Matheson, the Fuller brush salesman, was called Bristles; and curious Don McNeil, who was always in his window, was nicknamed Geranium. The folks in the photo are Norman Bethune Jr., "Wild" Angus McLeod, and Murdock "The Bishop" McAskill, who received his moniker because of his involvement at Greenwood Church.

In an article in *Outlook* magazine, published in December 1895, author William Ellsworth wrote of his experience with Baddeck nicknames during a trip to Cape Breton a year earlier: "There are forty John McLeods in and around Baddeck, none of them known as John McLeod, but each having a nickname usually derived from some small incident in his life. There is one who is associated with a mortgage and he is known as 'Mortgage McLeod,' his eldest son being 'First Mortgage McLeod' and his next son 'Second Mortgage McLeod.'"

Canadian writer Hugh MacLennan, who lived for a number of years in Baddeck, wrote in his book, *Rivers of Canada*, of a hilarious incident that earned one village boy a nickname for life. Seated in class at the Baddeck Academy, he simply responded to the teacher's question, "What does a cow have four of that I only have two of?" He was known forever after as "Neily Tits."

AFTERMATH OF A FIRE AT BETHUNE'S GARAGE, DECEMBER 1939

A week before Christmas in 1939, suppers were in the oven and life was humming when the lights went out. Suddenly, the darkness and quiet engulfed each house connected to the electrical wires that fed them power.

There had been occasional fires in the generators that powered the town before, but this time it was bad. This one refused to be extinguished. By the time the raging fire was finally snuffed out, the garage was in shambles and Norman Bethune's businesses were gone. The new cars, a well-stocked warehouse, and a sawmill were lost in the fire. It was a hard winter, but by mid-January, the power was restored, and later that year, the garage reopened.

SAILORS AT BRAS D'OR YACHT CLUB, C.1940   A number of these happy sailors are wearing shirts with the Northern Yacht Club (North Sydney) logo, but only a few have been identified. The man sitting on the far left in the front row is Gerald "Buddy" Dunlop (1921–2003).

Buddy, son of Bessie (McAskill) and Gerald Dunlop, loved the water and was an avid sailor. He was a member of the Bras d'Or Yacht Club for fifty-five years, and served as commodore from 1960 to 1972. Buddy was the fourth generation of the Dunlop family to operate the Telegraph House.

Front row, left to right: Buddy Dunlop, unidentified, Ray Kennedy, unidentified, unidentified, Fred Evans. *Middle row, left to right*: Sid Forsey, Owen Bryden, Lawton Icherwood, unidentified, unidentified, unidentified, Walter McKinley, unidentified. *Back row, left to right*: Steve Astephen, unidentified, unidentified, unidentified, unidentified, "Happy" Henderson, unidentified, unidentified, unidentified, Dan MacKenzie, Art Rooney.

Lobster boil, 1943

In the middle of World War II, peace was found on the shores of the Bras d'Or at a summer lobster boil on Kidston Island. *Back row, left to right*: Anna (Currie) McCarthy, Muriel (Carmichael) Bethune; *front row, left to right*: Nancy (MacDermid) Langley, Shirley (Dunlop) Kerr, Patsy (O'Toole) McManus. Peggy (MacDonald) Morrison may be the photographer.

For more than sixty years, these girls were friends. This photo, tucked in an album after Muriel Bethune's death in 2004, was simply described as "The Gang." Through the decades this group met after school, at weddings, bridge games, and baby showers, and shared each grand moment and small detail of their lives.

These enterprising Baddeck business-men were official Rotarians for only four-and-a-half years, but during that time their good deeds changed the face of the village.

They proposed a thirty-five-bed hospital for Baddeck and area and raised seven thousand dollars towards its construction. They purchased Alderwood, the former McCurdy homestead, for four thousand dollars, and donated the building to the municipality on the condition that it would be used as a home for the county's seniors.

In addition to these big projects, they looked after individuals in need, helping to pay the rent for a man who would otherwise be homeless, and providing eyeglasses for a number of county schoolchildren. The club hosted a number of well-known personalities, including premier Angus L. MacDonald, *National Geographic's*

BADDECK ROTARY CLUB, 1945

Gilbert Grosvenor, and Walter Plummer, the submarine commander who sank the first German warship in World War II (and was also a member of the club).

While the Rotary Club had lofty goals, the burden of raising money in such a small area became daunting. "I think we were too ambitious," Charles McCurdy commented in 1949, as he wrote to Rotary International to formally dissolve the Baddeck club. "The members in this small place could not stand the strain…(but) our Baddeck Rotary Club did a great deal of good."

Left to right, front row: Norman Bethune, Murdock McDermid, Charles McCurdy, Harry Stopford; *second row:* Bannington McAskill, J. C. Nicholson, James McKinnon, William McLeod; *third row:* George P. Fraser, Roddie Bethune, Harold Hall, Gordon S. Harvey, Reverend A. W. R. MacKenzie; *fourth row:* John D. McNeil, Johnnie Sam Campbell, Walter Plummer, Gordon MacAulay; *fifth row:* Walter Pinaud, James Fraser, Reverend R. A. Patterson.

This waterfront rink hosted friendly hockey games from morning until night in the 1940s and 1950s.

The players are to the west of the government wharf, with the freight shed in the background and the Baddeck Creamery to the left. In the 1950s a permanent outdoor rink was built on Ross Street, near the present-day Legion. In the 1970s the Victoria Highlands Civic Centre was built on Campbell Street, bringing hockey indoors.

CARS LINED ON ICE,
c.1950

The frozen Bras d'Or Lake provided a perfect track for horse racing. In the 1940s and 1950s, cars lined the track to watch as riders in sulkies raced on a straight track. Victoria County doctor C. L. "Monty" MacMillan and businessman James P. Fraser often jockeyed their own horses. By the 1950s, horse racing on the ice was a long-held tradition for Baddeck residents.

In the March 29, 1899, edition of the *Baddeck Telephone*, editor Charles Peppy wrote that spectators were on the ice "watching local trotters taking advantage of the '*glib*' (ice)." The course ran from the old Presbyterian Church (Bay Road) to Victoria Pier (near the government wharf). Peppy reported that on this particular day two of the four horses running were named Maud. The race ended with the Mauds placing first and second.

IDA AND MARGARET, 1916

This photo is addressed to Mary (Jones) Bethune, Dr. J. L.'s wife, and is dated August 21, 1916. The inscription reads:

> For Mrs. Bethune,
> The camera did not break and here is the result.
> Ida and Margaret.

Bibliography

BOOKS

Bascom, Robert O. *The Fort Edward Book.* Originally published by James Keating, 1903. Reprinted by Higginson Book Company, Massachusetts.

Berton, Pierre. *The Arctic Grail: The Quest for the Northwest Passage and the North Pole 1818–1909.* Toronto: McClelland and Stewart, 1988.

Bruce, Robert. *Alexander Graham Bell and the Conquest of Solitude.* Ithaca: Cornell University Press, 1973.

Campbell, Colin McDowall. *The Colonial Campbells, A Family History.* Hobart, Tasmania: Rothamay Press, 1984.

Flick, Alexander Clarence. *Loyalism in New York During the American Revolution.* Originally published by Columbia University Press, 1901. Reprinted by Kessinger Publishing.

Fuller, Mac. *Sparks and Volunteers.* Yarmouth: Sentinel Printing, 1997.

Green, H. Gordon. *The Silver Dart.* Fredericton: Brunswick Press, 1959.

Guttridge, Leonard G. *Ghosts of Cape Sabine.* New York: G. P. Putnam's Sons, 2000.

Ketchum, Richard M. *Saratoga.* New York: Henry Holt & Company, 1997.

Leavitt, Robert M. *Mi'kmaq of the East Coast.* Markham: Fitzhenry & Whiteside, 2000.

MacDonald, James W. *Honour Roll of the Nova Scotia Overseas Highland Brigade.* Sydney: Cape Breton University Press, 2007.

MacGreggor, Francis. *Days that I Remember: Stories with a Scottish Accent.* Hantsport: Lancelot Press, 1976.

MacMillan, C. Lamont. *Memoirs of a County Doctor.* Halifax: The Book Room, 1993.

McNeil, Neil. *The Highland Heart in Nova Scotia.* Wreck Cove: Breton Books, 1998.

McRae, Helen Fraser. *A Tiger on Dragon Mountain.* Prince Edward Island: Williams & Crue, 1993.

Nicholson, John A. et al. *Middle River Past and Present History of a Cape Breton Community 1806–1985.* Sydney: City Printers, 1985.

Parker, John. *Cape Breton Ships and Men.* England: Hazell Watson & Viney Ltd, 1967.

Patterson, George. *Patterson's History of Victoria County.* Sydney: College of Cape Breton Press, 1978.

Perry, Hattie A. *Old Days Old Ways: Early 20th Century Nova Scotia.* Tantallon: Four East Publications, 1989.

Todd, Alden. *Abandoned: The Story of the Greely Arctic Expedition 1881–1884.* Fairbanks: University of Alaska Press, 2001.

Thornhill, Bonnie, ed. *The Road to St. Ann's—An rathad gu bagh Naoimh Anna.* Englishtown: Victoria County Historical Society, 2007.

Thornhill, Bonnie, and James MacDonald. *In The Morning.* Sydney: University College of Cape Breton Press, 1999.

Toward, Lilias. *Mabel Bell, Alexander's Silent Partner.* Agincourt: Methuen, 1984.

Warner, Charles Dudley. *Baddeck And That Sort of Thing.* Cambridge: Riverside Press, 1874. Reprinted 1902.

UNPUBLISHED PAPERS AND MANUSCRIPTS

Bell, Alexander Graham and Mabel Hubbard Bell. Letters, diaries, notes, 1885–1923. Alexander Graham Bell National Historic Site, Baddeck, NS.

Campbell, Donald, and McLean, R. A. "Beyond the Atlantic Roar: A Study of the Nova Scotia Scot." 1974.

Elmsley, Robert. Elmsley's diary, an unpublished journal of life in Baddeck from 1840–1889.

Jones, Jonathan. Evidence on the claim of Jonathan Jones, personal letters written by Jones. The Beaton Institute, Cape Breton University.

Kennan, George. "Baddeck Public Library: Historical Sketch of the Origin and Growth of the Library 1981–1900." Abstract of a report made by the retiring president at the annual meeting of the trustees on November 19, 1900.

MacLean, Alex D. "The Early History of St. Michael's Parish." Baddeck, 1944.

Sparling, Florence. "Some Early Baddeckers: A genealogy of the Sparlings and Elmsleys." 1975.